Software-Defined Networking (SDN) with OpenStack

Leverage the best SDN technologies for your
OpenStack-based cloud infrastructure

Sriram Subramanian
Sreenivas Voruganti

BIRMINGHAM - MUMBAI

Software-Defined Networking (SDN) with OpenStack

First published: October 2016

Production reference: 1211016

Published by Packt Publishing Ltd.

Livery Place

35 Livery Street

Birmingham B3 2PB, UK.

ISBN 978-1-78646-599-3

www.packtpub.com

Credits

Authors

Sriram Subramanian
Sreenivas Voruganti

Reviewer

Alberto Morgante Medina

Commissioning Editor

Kartikey Pandey

Acquisition Editor

Prachi Bisht

Content Development Editor

Divij Kotian

Technical Editor

Shivani K. Mistry

Copy Editor

Safis Editing

Project Coordinator

Sheejal Shah

Proofreader

Safis Editing

Indexer

Rekha Nair

Production Coordinator

Melwyn Dsa

Cover Work

Melwyn Dsa

About the Authors

Sriram Subramanian is an experienced professional with over 19 years' experience of building networking and network management products. Since 2011, Sriram has been working with Juniper Networks, leading engineering teams responsible for OpenStack Neutron plugins, VMware integration, and network management products. He is a technologist with a passion for virtualization and cloud networking. Sriram blogs regularly at `http://www.innervoice.in/blogs` and loves experimenting with new technologies and programming. He is the author of *OpenStack Networking Cookbook, Packt*.

I would like to dedicate this book to my family. I want to thank my wife, Kala, for her support during this entire project. Her "give your best" attitude motivates me to strive harder in managing my time and energy effectively. I also want to thank Appa and Amma for their patience and blessings. And a special thank you to my daughter Navya and our labrador Neige for the joie de vivre they bring to my life.

I extend a special thank you to my employer, Juniper Networks, and specifically my manager, Rakesh Manocha. The leadership team at Juniper has created an environment where individuals can pursue excellence through innovation. It has helped me expand my knowledge and capabilities beyond my imagination.

I would like to express my gratitude to my publishers, Packt and the reviewers, who provided invaluable feedback. Thanks to Divij Kotian, our editor, who played a crucial role keeping this book project on track. Finally, a big thank you to Sreeni for being a great co-author and partner on this exciting book journey.

Sreenivas Voruganti is presently driving IoT solutions at Aricent. He previously led engineering teams responsible for building networking, wireless LAN, and SDN products at Juniper Networks. He has contributed to building a range of IP and ATM-based Telco products at Lucent Technologies, Tellabs, and BHEL.

He is an avid student of emerging trends in networking and virtualization technologies and is passionate about integrating them to deliver solutions. His current interests include IoT, SDN, and NFV.

He is an inventor and has US Patent grants on networking, QoS, and wireless.

What started as an idea over coffee has come to form thanks to Sriram's drive and insightful ideas on book writing. Thanks, Sriram, for all the fun times working together.

I would like to dedicate this book to my parents for their blessings and wishes, to my wife, Nimmi, and sons, Aaditya and Arjun, for unstinting support through this endeavor.

Thanks to Alberto for valuable review comments, Divij Kotian, our editor, for fantastic support, Shivani for great job in editing the content, and our publishers Packt.

Finally, a big thank you to all the folks who contributed to the SDN open source implementations and friends who helped refine my understanding.

About the Reviewer

Alberto Morgante Medina is an engineer who's passionate about cloud computing. He loves new technologies, and he thinks that SecDevOps is the way to improve and apply them. He's always looking for new challenges. He has been working on OpenStack, several SDN solutions, information security, and other related IT areas since 2010. He is currently working at BBVA Bank as an innovation engineer. Before that, he worked at Telefónica as a cloud computing and security engineer.

www.PacktPub.com

For support files and downloads related to your book, please visit www.PacktPub.com.

Did you know that Packt offers eBook versions of every book published, with PDF and ePub files available? You can upgrade to the eBook version at www.PacktPub.com and as a print book customer, you are entitled to a discount on the eBook copy. Get in touch with us at service@packtpub.com for more details.

At www.PacktPub.com, you can also read a collection of free technical articles, sign up for a range of free newsletters and receive exclusive discounts and offers on Packt books and eBooks.

https://www.packtpub.com/mapt

Get the most in-demand software skills with Mapt. Mapt gives you full access to all Packt books and video courses, as well as industry-leading tools to help you plan your personal development and advance your career.

Why subscribe?

- Fully searchable across every book published by Packt
- Copy and paste, print, and bookmark content
- On demand and accessible via a web browser

Table of Contents

Preface

OpenStack is rapidly becoming the prominent open source platform for building public and private clouds. OpenStack-based clouds are built on three important pillars, namely, compute, storage, and networking. The strength of these pillars determines the robustness, scale, and performance of your OpenStack cloud.

The classic networking landscape is changing, with SDN approach to building networks becoming mainstream, backed by superior economics and the fact that it is a platform for innovation. We believe that the SDN application space will only grow bigger, with innovative applications that are currently in their infancy and it is essentially replacing the conventional network application with the SDN approach.

With both OpenStack and SDN poised for rapid adoption, it is important to understand the key technologies at their intersection. The intent of the book is to provide an overview of the key SDN technologies and their relevance with respect to OpenStack, in a simple and easy to understand format to encourage the reader to dig into the details for deeper insights.

What this book covers

Chapter 1, *OpenStack Networking in a Nutshell*, provides an overview of OpenStack Networking using Neutron. After introducing core networking constructs such as network, subnet, and port, the chapter will highlight different networking services within OpenStack such as routing, firewall, and VPN.

Chapter 2, *Introduction to Software-Defined Networking*, introduces the readers to the concepts related to software-defined network. We will look at the challenges in traditional networking, especially in the rapidly evolving cloud infrastructure use case. We introduce different SDN's concepts by highlighting the advantages of traditional networking.

Chapter 3, *SDN Protocols*, delves into the underlying components and protocols that enable the SDN-based architecture. We will introduce Open vSwitch (OVS), a popular virtual switch in SDN and OpenStack environments and help you gain insights into SDN building blocks.

Chapter 4, *SDN Networking with Open vSwitch,* begins with lightweight virtual networking with a Linux network namespace and Open vSwitch functioning as a conventional L2 switch. We will then bring OpenFlow into the mix to depict flow-based networking with virtual machines, interfacing with SDN controller. We will introduce Mininet, a network emulation tool for prototyping network topologies. Finally, we will depict the architecture of Neutron, the networking component of OpenStack.

Chapter 5, *Getting Started with OpenDaylight,* will help the user get started with OpenDaylight (ODL) as an SDN technology. From an architectural overview of installation and configuration, the goal of this chapter is to give the readers a high-level overview of ODL.

Chapter 6, *Using OpenDaylight with OpenStack,* will cover ODL-based network service provisioning in OpenStack. Starting with simple multi-tenant virtual networks, the chapter will move on to advanced services such as load balancers and service chaining using ODL. We will also show high-level APIs and the programmability of ODL.

Chapter 7, *Getting Started with OpenContrail,* helps the user get started with OpenContrail as an SDN technology. From an architectural overview of installation and configuration, the goal of this chapter is to give the audience a high-level overview of OpenContrail.

Chapter 8, *OpenContrail Networking with OpenStack,* explains OpenStack and OpenContrail integration. Starting with simple multi-tenant overlay networks, the chapter will move on to advanced services, such as security and service chaining using OpenContrail.

Chapter 9, *Open Network Operating System (ONOS),* starts with an introduction to ONOS its architecture, and then explores ONOS integration with Open vSwitch (OVS). We will conclude the chapter with a quick introduction to using ONOS in an OpenStack environment.

Chapter 10, *OVN and Open vSwitch Enhancements,* outlines the limitations in the classic Neutron architecture and covers solutions such as OVN, Distributed Virtual Router (DVR), Dragonflow, and Open vSwitch Data Path Development Kit (OVS-DPDK). The chapter covers how OVN integrates with OpenStack and the mapping of their object model.

What you need for this book

While SDN is being driven by solutions both from vibrant open source community and from networking vendors we focused on leveraging the open source software with a hands-on approach to gaining technology and implementation insights. You will need computers or servers running on a Intel x86 processor with VT extensions, at least 4 GB RAM and 100 GB HDD. Each computer will require at least three network interfaces.

Considering the rapid updates to technology and implementation we strongly recommend following the relevant links supplied for topics for further reading.

Who this book is for

The target audience for this book is system and network administrators, IT data center managers, cloud infrastructure providers, and users of private and public clouds. It will also be a good introduction for networking enthusiasts.

The readers are assumed to have a very basic knowledge of OpenStack, networking, and Linux. Armed with the basic knowledge, this book will help the readers get an overview of popular SDN technologies and how these are used in an OpenStack-based cloud infrastructure.

Conventions

In this book, you will find a number of text styles that distinguish between different kinds of information. Here are some examples of these styles and an explanation of their meaning.

Code words in text, database table names, folder names, filenames, file extensions, pathnames, dummy URLs, user input, and Twitter handles are shown as follows: "The neutron `firewall-create` command supports an option to pick a specific router as well."

Any command-line input or output is written as follows:

```
$ sudo apt-get install openvswitch
```

New terms and **important words** are shown in bold. Words that you see on the screen, for example, in menus or dialog boxes, appear in the text like this: "In the left navigation bar, click on the **Nodes**."

Warnings or important notes appear in a box like this.

 Tips and tricks appear like this.

Reader feedback

Feedback from our readers is always welcome. Let us know what you think about this book—what you liked or disliked. Reader feedback is important for us as it helps us develop titles that you will really get the most out of.

To send us general feedback, simply e-mail `feedback@packtpub.com`, and mention the book's title in the subject of your message.

If there is a topic that you have expertise in and you are interested in either writing or contributing to a book, see our author guide at `www.packtpub.com/authors`.

Customer support

Now that you are the proud owner of a Packt book, we have a number of things to help you to get the most from your purchase.

Downloading the color images of this book

We also provide you with a PDF file that has color images of the screenshots/diagrams used in this book. The color images will help you better understand the changes in the output. You can download this file from `https://www.packtpub.com/sites/default/files/down loads/SoftwareDefinedNetworkingwithOpenStack_ColorImages.pdf`.

Errata

Although we have taken every care to ensure the accuracy of our content, mistakes do happen. If you find a mistake in one of our books—maybe a mistake in the text or the code—we would be grateful if you could report this to us. By doing so, you can save other readers from frustration and help us improve subsequent versions of this book. If you find any errata, please report them by visiting http://www.packtpub.com/submit-errata, selecting your book, clicking on the **Errata Submission Form** link, and entering the details of your errata. Once your errata are verified, your submission will be accepted and the errata will be uploaded to our website or added to any list of existing errata under the Errata section of that title.

To view the previously submitted errata, go to https://www.packtpub.com/books/content/support and enter the name of the book in the search field. The required information will appear under the **Errata** section.

Piracy

Piracy of copyrighted material on the Internet is an ongoing problem across all media. At Packt, we take the protection of our copyright and licenses very seriously. If you come across any illegal copies of our works in any form on the Internet, please provide us with the location address or website name immediately so that we can pursue a remedy.

Please contact us at copyright@packtpub.com with a link to the suspected pirated material.

We appreciate your help in protecting our authors and our ability to bring you valuable content.

Questions

If you have a problem with any aspect of this book, you can contact us at questions@packtpub.com, and we will do our best to address the problem.

1
OpenStack Networking in a Nutshell

Information technology (IT) applications are rapidly moving from dedicated infrastructure to a dynamic cloud-based infrastructure. This move to cloud started with server virtualization, where a hardware server ran as a virtual machine on a hypervisor. The adoption of cloud-based applications has accelerated due to factors such as globalization and outsourcing, where diverse teams need to collaborate in real time.

Server hardware connects to network switches using Ethernet and IP to establish network connectivity. However, as servers move from physical to virtual, the network boundary also moves from the physical network to the virtual network. Traditionally, applications, servers, and networking were tightly integrated. But modern enterprises and IT infrastructure demand flexibility in order to support complex applications.

The flexibility of cloud infrastructure requires networking to be dynamic and scalable. **Software-Defined Networking (SDN)** and **Network Function Virtualization (NFV)** play a critical role in data centers in order to deliver the flexibility and agility demanded by cloud-based applications. By providing practical management tools and abstractions that hide the underlying physical network's complexity, SDN allows operators to build complex networking capabilities on demand.

OpenStack is an open source cloud platform that helps build public and private cloud at scale. Within OpenStack, the name for the OpenStack Networking project is Neutron. The functionality of Neutron can be classified as *core* and *service*.

This chapter aims to provide a short introduction to OpenStack Networking. We will cover the following topics in this chapter:

- Understanding traffic flows between virtual and physical networks
- Neutron entities that support Layer 2 (L2) networking
- Layer 3 (L3) or routing between OpenStack networks
- Securing OpenStack network traffic
- Advanced networking services in OpenStack
- OpenStack and SDN

The terms Neutron and OpenStack Networking are used interchangeably throughout this book.

Virtual and physical networking

Server virtualization led to the adoption of virtualized applications and workloads running inside physical servers. While physical servers are connected to the physical network equipment, modern networking has pushed the boundary of networks into the virtual domain as well. Virtual switches, firewalls, and routers play a critical role in the flexibility provided by cloud infrastructure:

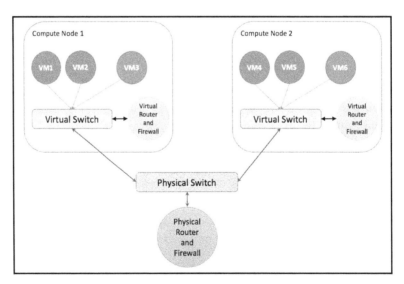

Figure 1: Networking components for server virtualization

The preceding diagram describes a typical virtualized server and its various networking components.

The virtual machines are connected to a **Virtual Switch** inside the **Compute Node** (or server). The traffic is secured using virtual routers and firewalls. The **Compute Node** is connected to a **Physical Switch**, which is the entry point into the physical network.

Let us now walk through different traffic flow scenarios using *Figure 1* as the background. In *Figure 2*, traffic from one VM to another on the same **Compute Node** is forwarded by the **Virtual Switch** itself. It does not reach the physical network. You can even apply firewall rules to traffic between the two virtual machines:

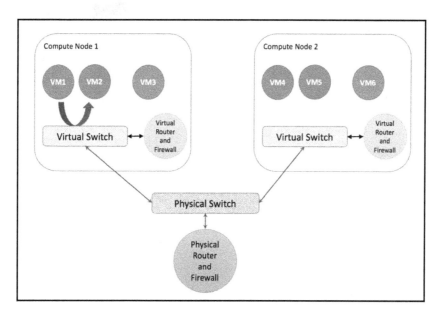

Figure 2: Traffic flow between two virtual machines on the same server

Next, let us have a look at how traffic flows between virtual machines across two compute nodes. In *Figure 3*, the traffic comes out from the first **Compute Node** and then reaches the **Physical Switch**. The **Physical Switch** forwards the traffic to the second **Compute Node** and the **Virtual Switch** within the second **Compute Node** steers the traffic to the appropriate **VM**:

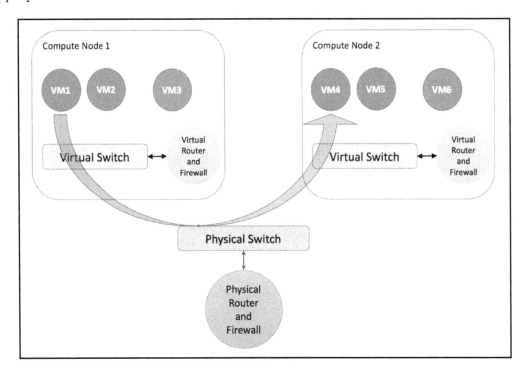

Figure 3: Traffic flow between two virtual machines on different servers

Finally, the following diagram is a depiction of traffic flow when a virtual machine sends or receives traffic from the Internet. The **Physical Switch** forwards the traffic to the **Physical Router and Firewall,** which is presumed to be connected to the Internet:

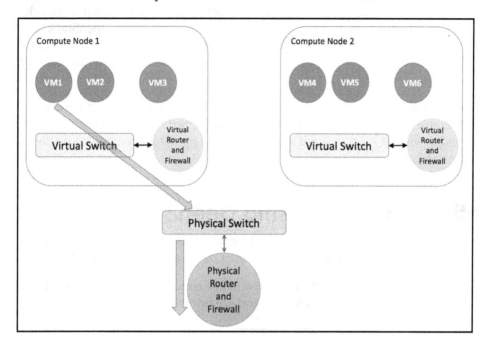

Figure 4: Traffic flow from a virtual machine to external network

As seen in the preceding diagrams, the physical and the virtual network components work together to provide connectivity to virtual machines and applications.

Tenant isolation

As a cloud platform, OpenStack supports multiple users grouped into *tenants*. One of the key requirements of a multi-tenant cloud is to provide isolation of data traffic belonging to one tenant from the rest of the tenants that use the same infrastructure. OpenStack supports different ways of achieving the isolation of network data traffic and it is the responsibility of the virtual switch on each compute node to implement the isolation.

Layer 2 (L2) capabilities in OpenStack

In networking terminology, the connectivity to a physical or virtual switch is also known as Layer 2 (L2) connectivity. L2 connectivity is the most fundamental form of network connectivity needed for virtual machines. As mentioned previously, OpenStack supports *core* and *service* functionality. The L2 connectivity for virtual machines falls under the core capability of OpenStack Networking, whereas router, firewall, and so on fall under the service category.

The L2 connectivity in OpenStack is realized using two constructs, called **network** and **subnet**. Operators can use OpenStack CLI or the web interface to create networks and subnets. And as virtual machines are instantiated, the operators can associate them to appropriate networks.

Creating a network using OpenStack CLI

A network defines the Layer 2 (L2) boundary for all the instances that are associated with it. All the virtual machines within a network are part of the same L2 broadcast domain.

The Liberty release has introduced a new OpenStack **command-line interface** (**CLI**) for different services. We will use the new CLI and see how to create a network:

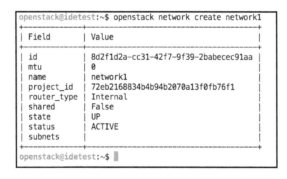

```
openstack@idetest:~$ openstack network create network1
+-------------+--------------------------------------+
| Field       | Value                                |
+-------------+--------------------------------------+
| id          | 8d2f1d2a-cc31-42f7-9f39-2babecec91aa |
| mtu         | 0                                    |
| name        | network1                             |
| project_id  | 72eb2168834b4b94b2070a13f0fb76f1     |
| router_type | Internal                             |
| shared      | False                                |
| state       | UP                                   |
| status      | ACTIVE                               |
| subnets     |                                      |
+-------------+--------------------------------------+
openstack@idetest:~$
```

Creating a subnet using OpenStack CLI

A subnet is a range of IP addresses that are assigned to virtual machines on the associated Network. OpenStack Neutron configures a DHCP server with this IP address range and it starts one DHCP server instance per network, by default.

We will now show you how to create a subnet using OpenStack CLI:

> Unlike a network, for a subnet, we need to use the regular *Neutron* CLI command in the Liberty release.

```
openstack@idetest:~$ neutron subnet-create --name subnet1 network1 192.168.20.0/24
Created a new subnet:
+------------------+-----------------------------------------------+
| Field            | Value                                         |
+------------------+-----------------------------------------------+
| allocation_pools | {"start": "192.168.20.2", "end": "192.168.20.254"} |
| cidr             | 192.168.20.0/24                               |
| dns_nameservers  |                                               |
| enable_dhcp      | True                                          |
| gateway_ip       | 192.168.20.1                                  |
| host_routes      |                                               |
| id               | e9aa6a23-bf66-4854-8d7d-ebf7e65426e7          |
| ip_version       | 4                                             |
| ipv6_address_mode |                                              |
| ipv6_ra_mode     |                                               |
| name             | subnet1                                       |
| network_id       | 8d2f1d2a-cc31-42f7-9f39-2babecec91aa          |
| subnetpool_id    |                                               |
| tenant_id        | 72eb2168834b4b94b2070a13f0fb76f1              |
+------------------+-----------------------------------------------+
```

Associating a network and subnet to a virtual machine

To give a complete perspective, we will create a virtual machine using the OpenStack web interface and show you how to associate a network and subnet to a virtual machine.

In your OpenStack web interface, navigate to **Project** | **Compute** | **Instances**:

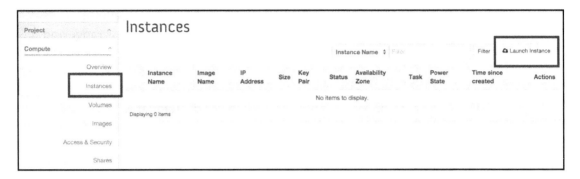

Click on the **Launch Instance** action on the right-hand side, as highlighted in the preceding screenshot. In the resulting window, enter the name for your instance and how you want to boot your instance:

To associate a network and a subnet with the instance, click on the **Networking** tab. If you have more than one tenant network, you will be able to choose the network you want to associate with the instance. If you have exactly one network, the web interface will automatically select it:

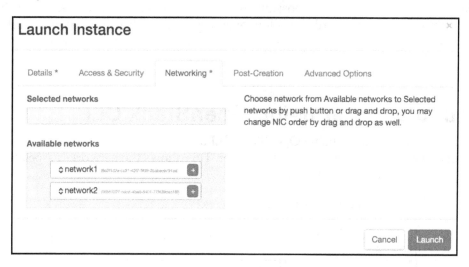

As mentioned previously, providing isolation for tenant network traffic is a key requirement for any cloud. OpenStack Neutron uses network and subnet to define the boundaries and isolate data traffic between different tenants. Depending on Neutron configuration, the actual isolation of traffic is accomplished by the virtual switches. VLAN and VXLAN are the most common networking technologies used to isolate traffic, in addition to protocols such as GRE.

Layer 3 (L3) capabilities in OpenStack

Once L2 connectivity is established, the virtual machines within one network can send or receive traffic between themselves. However, two virtual machines belonging to two different networks will not be able to communicate with each other automatically. This is done to provide privacy and isolation for tenant networks. In order to allow traffic from one Network to reach another network, OpenStack Networking supports an entity called a router.

The default implementation of OpenStack uses *namespaces* to support L3 routing capabilities. Namespaces are networking constructs in Linux that allow you to create a copy of the TCP/IP network stack all the way from the Ethernet interfaces (L2), routing tables, and so on, such that each instance is isolated from the other. In a cloud environment (especially for multi-tenancy), it is possible that users use the same IP addresses for their virtual machine instances. In order to allow overlapping IP addresses to co-exist within the same infrastructure, Neutron uses network namespaces to provide the isolation between overlapping IP addresses.

Creating a router using OpenStack CLI

Operators can create routers using OpenStack CLI or web interface. They can then add more than one subnet as an *interface* to the router. This allows the networks associated with the router to exchange traffic with one another.

The command to create a router is as follows:

```
openstack@idetest:~$ neutron router-create router1
Created a new router:
+-----------------------+--------------------------------------+
| Field                 | Value                                |
+-----------------------+--------------------------------------+
| admin_state_up        | True                                 |
| external_gateway_info |                                      |
| id                    | 0bb735b9-de1c-4b32-b3e8-e24331d84084 |
| name                  | router1                              |
| routes                |                                      |
| status                | ACTIVE                               |
| tenant_id             | 72eb2168834b4b94b2070a13f0fb76f1     |
+-----------------------+--------------------------------------+
```

This command creates a router with the specified name.

Associating a subnetwork to a Router

Once a router is created, the next step is to associate one or more subnetworks to the router. The command to accomplish this is as follows:

```
openstack@idetest:~$ neutron router-interface-add router1 subnet1
Added interface fb931c09-ca59-4196-8829-9d34107e5b9d to router router1.
```

The subnet represented by **subnet1** is now associated to the router **router1**. Using the OpenStack dashboard, you can view the association between a router and a subnet. Navigate to **Project | Networks | Network Topology**. This should display the router, **router1**, connected to the network, **network1**, to which the subnet belongs, as shown in the following screenshot:

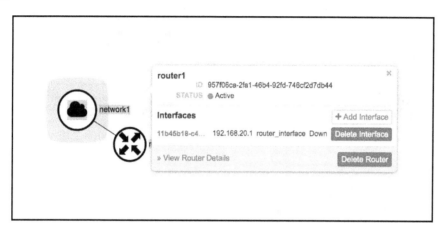

You can hover the mouse over the router **router1** to see that the subnet is indeed added as an interface and is assigned an IP address.

Securing network traffic in OpenStack

The security of network traffic is critical, and OpenStack supports two mechanisms to secure network traffic. *Security Groups* allow traffic within a tenant's network to be secured. Linux *iptables* on the compute nodes are used to implement OpenStack security groups.

The traffic that goes outside of a tenant's network, to another network or the Internet, is secured using the OpenStack firewall service functionality. Like routing, firewall is a service with Neutron. The firewall service also uses iptables, but the scope of iptables is limited to the OpenStack router used as part of the firewall service.

The following diagram describes at a high level how iptables are used to secure network traffic:

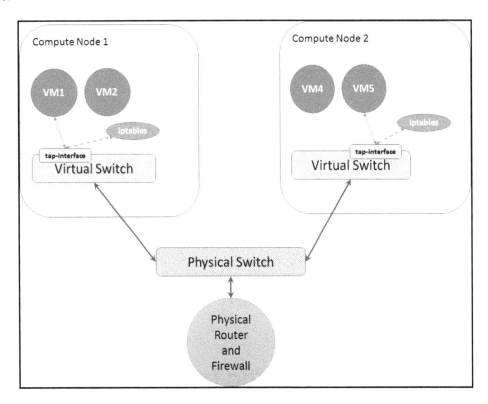

In this network diagram, the **VM** instances are connected to the **Virtual Switch** using **tap-interface**. The security group's rules to allow or deny data traffic are mapped to **iptables** rules on the compute nodes. The **iptables** rules operate on these **tap-interface** to ensure that traffic is allowed or blocked as per the configured rules.

Using security groups to secure traffic within a network

In order to secure traffic going from one VM to another *within* a given network, we must create a security group. The command to create a security group is as follows:

```
openstack@idetest:~$ openstack security group create security_group_1
+-------------+------------------------------------------+
| Field       | Value                                    |
+-------------+------------------------------------------+
| description | security_group_1                         |
| id          | 0831338a-17b7-48dc-8e2a-c08aadb2f8a6     |
| name        | security_group_1                         |
| rules       | []                                       |
| tenant_id   | 47040f6c27db41ec8edaafdcae25fc98         |
+-------------+------------------------------------------+
```

The next step is to create one or more rules within the security group. As an example, let us create a rule which allows only UDP, incoming traffic on port 8080 from any source IP address:

```
openstack@idetest:~$ openstack security group rule create --proto udp \
> --dst-port 8080:8080 security_group_1
+----------------+------------------------------------------+
| Field          | Value                                    |
+----------------+------------------------------------------+
| group          | {}                                       |
| id             | d24d8f05-5730-49bd-ae7d-2576d84800b8     |
| ip_protocol    | udp                                      |
| ip_range       | 0.0.0.0/0                                |
| parent_group_id| 0831338a-17b7-48dc-8e2a-c08aadb2f8a6     |
| port_range     | 8080:8080                                |
+----------------+------------------------------------------+
```

The final step is to associate this security group and the rules to a virtual machine instance. We will use the `nova boot` command for this:

```
openstack@idetest:~$ nova boot --flavor m1.tiny \
> --image cirros-0.3.4-x86_64-uec \
> --security-groups security_group_1 \
> vm1
+-------------------------------------+--------------------------------------------------------------+
| Property                            | Value                                                        |
+-------------------------------------+--------------------------------------------------------------+
| OS-DCF:diskConfig                   | MANUAL                                                       |
| OS-EXT-AZ:availability_zone         |                                                              |
| OS-EXT-STS:power_state              | 0                                                            |
| OS-EXT-STS:task_state               | scheduling                                                   |
| OS-EXT-STS:vm_state                 | building                                                     |
| OS-SRV-USG:launched_at              | -                                                            |
| OS-SRV-USG:terminated_at            | -                                                            |
| accessIPv4                          |                                                              |
| accessIPv6                          |                                                              |
| adminPass                           | gRtuYD94ppbD                                                 |
| config_drive                        |                                                              |
| created                             | 2016-03-16T05:37:16Z                                         |
| flavor                              | m1.tiny (1)                                                  |
| hostId                              |                                                              |
| id                                  | a08aa651-b823-41a5-b1bd-997098f92ab7                         |
| image                               | cirros-0.3.4-x86_64-uec (838814fe-b40d-40ac-8558-6cf1b0e208a5)|
| key_name                            | -                                                            |
| metadata                            | {}                                                           |
| name                                | vm1                                                          |
| os-extended-volumes:volumes_attached| []                                                           |
| progress                            | 0                                                            |
| security_groups                     | security_group_1                                             |
| status                              | BUILD                                                        |
| tenant_id                           | 47040f6c27db41ec8edaafdcae25fc98                             |
| updated                             | 2016-03-16T05:37:16Z                                         |
| user_id                             | e3ecda85bb194a469328a9b35cbdda03                             |
+-------------------------------------+--------------------------------------------------------------+
```

Once the virtual machine instance has a security group associated with it, the incoming traffic will be monitored and depending upon the rules inside the security group, data traffic may be blocked or permitted to reach the virtual machine.

 It is possible to block ingress or egress traffic using security groups.

Using firewall service to secure traffic

We have seen that security groups provide a fine grain control over what traffic is allowed to and from a virtual machine instance. Another layer of security supported by OpenStack is **Firewall as a Service** (**FWaaS**). FWaaS enforces security at the router level, whereas security groups enforce security at a virtual-machine-interface level.

The main use case of FWaaS is to protect *all* virtual machine instances *within* a network from threats and attacks from *outside* the network. This could be virtual machines part of another network in the same OpenStack cloud or some entity in the Internet trying to perform an unauthorized access.

Let's now see how FWaaS is used in OpenStack. In FWaaS, a set of firewall rules is grouped into a firewall policy and then a firewall is created that implements one policy at a time. This firewall is then associated to a router.

A firewall rule can be created using the `neutron firewall-rule-create` command, as follows:

```
openstack@idetest:~$ neutron firewall-rule-create --protocol icmp --action deny \
> --name BlockPingTraffic
Created a new firewall_rule:
+------------------------+--------------------------------------+
| Field                  | Value                                |
+------------------------+--------------------------------------+
| action                 | deny                                 |
| description            |                                      |
| destination_ip_address |                                      |
| destination_port       |                                      |
| enabled                | True                                 |
| firewall_policy_id     |                                      |
| id                     | 9081a8f1-6f03-48e0-952f-361667ccff09 |
| ip_version             | 4                                    |
| name                   | BlockPingTraffic                     |
| position               |                                      |
| protocol               | icmp                                 |
| shared                 | False                                |
| source_ip_address      |                                      |
| source_port            |                                      |
| tenant_id              | 1053380ae6244a38879281bc802fa2e0     |
+------------------------+--------------------------------------+
```

This rule blocks the ICMP protocol so applications such as `Ping` will be blocked by the firewall. The next step is to create a firewall policy. In real-world scenarios, the security administrators will define several rules and consolidate them under a single policy. For example, all rules that block various types of traffic can be combined into a single policy. The command to create a firewall policy is as follows:

```
openstack@idetest:~$ neutron firewall-policy-create \
> --firewall-rules BlockPingTraffic \
> BlockPolicy
Created a new firewall_policy:
+----------------+--------------------------------------+
| Field          | Value                                |
+----------------+--------------------------------------+
| audited        | False                                |
| description    |                                      |
| firewall_rules | 9081a8f1-6f03-48e0-952f-361667ccff09 |
| id             | 9fb0f008-ecc2-4f06-a5ee-6deee478e591 |
| name           | BlockPolicy                          |
| shared         | False                                |
| tenant_id      | 1053380ae6244a38879281bc802fa2e0     |
+----------------+--------------------------------------+
```

The final step is to create a firewall and associate it with a router. The command to do this is as follows:

```
openstack@idetest:~$ neutron firewall-create --name FinanceFirewall BlockPolicy
Created a new firewall:
+---------------------+------------------------------------------+
| Field               | Value                                    |
+---------------------+------------------------------------------+
| admin_state_up      | True                                     |
| description         |                                          |
| firewall_policy_id  | 9fb0f008-ecc2-4f06-a5ee-6deee478e591     |
| id                  | 9e6f784c-6bb9-477d-a40c-8701d1f2fd09     |
| name                | FinanceFirewall                          |
| router_ids          | 3ed7a392-bddd-4300-b33a-579c582a8d91     |
|                     | 6e529858-48ad-482e-a017-5e383be99730     |
| status              | PENDING_CREATE                           |
| tenant_id           | 1053380ae6244a38879281bc802fa2e0         |
+---------------------+------------------------------------------+
```

In the preceding command, we did not specify any routers and the OpenStack behavior is to associate the firewall (and in turn the policy and rules) to *all* the routers available for that tenant. The `neutron firewall-create` command supports an option to pick a specific router as well.

Advanced networking services

Besides routing and firewall, OpenStack supports a few other commonly used networking technologies. Let's take a quick look at these without delving too deep into the respective commands.

Load Balancing as a Service (LBaaS)

Virtual machine instances created in OpenStack are used to run applications. Most applications are required to support redundancy and concurrent access. For example, a web server may be accessed by a large number of users at the same time. One of the common strategies to handle scale and redundancy is to implement load balancing for incoming requests. In this approach, a **load balancer** distributes an incoming service request onto a pool of servers, which processes the request, thus providing higher throughput. If one of the servers in the pool fails, the load balancer removes it from the pool and the subsequent service requests are distributed among the remaining servers. Users of the application use the IP address of the load balancer to access the application and are unaware of the pool of servers.

OpenStack implements load balancing using *HAproxy* software and a Linux namespace.

Virtual Private Network as a Service (VPNaaS)

As mentioned previously, tenant isolation requires data traffic to be segregated and secured within an OpenStack cloud. However, there are times when external entities need to be part of the same network without removing the firewall-based security. This can be accomplished using a **Virtual Private Network** (**VPN**).

A VPN connects two endpoints on different networks over a public Internet connection, such that the endpoints appear to be directly connected to each other. VPNs also provide confidentiality and integrity of transmitted data.

Neutron provides a service plugin that enables OpenStack users to connect two networks using a VPN. The reference implementation of the VPN plugin in Neutron uses *Openswan* to create an IPSec-based VPN. IPSec is a suite of protocols that provides a secure connection between two endpoints by encrypting each IP packet transferred between them.

OpenStack and SDN context

So far in this chapter, we have seen the different networking capabilities provided by OpenStack. Let us now look at two capabilities in OpenStack that enable SDN to be leveraged effectively.

Choice of technology

OpenStack, being an open source platform, bundles open source networking solutions as the default implementation for these networking capabilities. For example, routing is supported using *namespace*, security using *iptables*, and load balancing using *HAproxy*.

Historically, these networking capabilities were implemented using customized hardware and software, most of them being proprietary solutions. These custom solutions are capable of much higher performance and are well-supported by their vendors. Hence they have a place in the OpenStack and SDN ecosystem.

From its initial releases, OpenStack has been designed for extensibility. Vendors can write their own extensions and then can easily configure OpenStack to use their extension instead of the default solutions. This allows operators to deploy the networking technology of their choice.

OpenStack API for networking

One of the most powerful capabilities of OpenStack is the extensive support for APIs. All OpenStack services interact with one another using well-defined RESTful APIs. This allows custom implementations and pluggable components to provide powerful enhancements for practical cloud implementation.

For example, when a network is created using the OpenStack web interface, a RESTful request is sent to the Horizon service. This in turn, invokes a RESTful API to validate the user using the Keystone service. Once validated, Horizon sends another RESTful API request to Neutron to actually create the network.

In the following chapter, we will see how these RESTful APIs provide support for crucial SDN capabilities in an OpenStack-based cloud.

Summary

As seen in this chapter, OpenStack supports a wide variety of networking functionality right out of the box. The importance of isolating tenant traffic and the need to allow customized solutions requires OpenStack to support flexible configuration. We also highlighted some key aspects of OpenStack that will play a key role in deploying SDN in data centers, thereby supporting powerful cloud architecture and solutions.

The following chapter will introduce SDN and demonstrate how it solves some of the challenges with traditional networking. We will examine how OpenStack and SDN together provide a modern cloud networking solution.

2
Introduction to Software-Defined Networking

As mentioned in the previous chapter, businesses and enterprises are moving towards newer architectures for building and deploying applications. With technologies such as virtualization and containerization, it is possible to rapidly deploy complex and highly scalable applications within an enterprise or on a public cloud or both.

Common IT applications require compute, storage, and networking resources. Traditionally, the server and storage infrastructure was installed and configured by system administrators and then separately, network administrators used to connect the servers and configure the network. This silo-based approach does not scale for today's on-demand and highly automated application deployment needs. Moreover, the traditional network architecture was designed for more static application environment, whereas flexibility is the need of the hour now.

This is where SDN comes into the picture. SDN makes the network infrastructure easier to manage and integrate with the server and storage infrastructure. As a result, the resources needed for application deployment can be provided in an agile yet flexible manner.

Let's now look at the definition of SDN. The **Open Networking Forum** (**ONF**) defines SDN as follows:

> *"Software-Defined Networking (SDN) is an emerging architecture that is dynamic, manageable, cost-effective, and adaptable, making it ideal for the high-bandwidth, dynamic nature of today's applications. This architecture decouples the network control and forwarding functions enabling the network control to become directly programmable and the underlying infrastructure to be abstracted for applications and network services. The OpenFlow protocol is a foundational element for building SDN solutions."*

The ONF definition specifically talks about the OpenFlow protocol and the decoupling of control and forwarding functions. But the key message in the definition is that SDN must support dynamic applications. It is possible to implement SDN using other protocols and technologies to meet the same goal.

In the rest of this chapter, we will delve deeper into SDN and show how OpenStack and SDN are related. We will cover the following topics in this chapter:

- Components of traditional networks
- Challenges faced by traditional networks
- SDN reference architecture
- SDN and OpenStack

Components of traditional networks

Let us start our deep dive into SDN by looking at the components of a network device. Networking functionality can be broadly classified into three *planes*. These are as follows:

- **Data plane**: The act of moving bits that constitute the packet from an incoming port to an outgoing port is the responsibility of the *data plane*. This is also known as the *forwarding plane*. For example, in Ethernet switches, packets coming in from one port are forwarded out via one or more of the remaining ports.
- **Control plane**: Using the previous example, to forward the packet to the correct outgoing port, the data plane may need additional information. In the case of Ethernet switches, the outgoing port is identified using the destination MAC address learnt by the switch. This act of *learning* and building *awareness* about the network is the responsibility of the control plane. The control plane learns and gathers information about the network using various protocols. In a switch, network loops are detected using the spanning tree protocol. In routing, the OSPF protocol helps in learning network topology. The important thing here is that the *data plane* leverages the information built by the *control plane*.
- **Management plane**: While networks do their job of processing and forwarding data traffic, it is important to monitor their health and configure them to suit your needs. This ability to manage and control a networking device is the responsibility of the *management plane*. The common mechanisms to manage networks include the command-line interface (CLI), SNMP protocol, and so on. RESTful API using HTTP has gained in popularity as a management plane protocol recently. Usually, network administrators are the end users of management plane capabilities.

The following diagram depicts the three planes of networking. The management plane is represented by the operator. The control plane encompasses more than one networking device, whereas the scope of data plane functions is limited to each networking device:

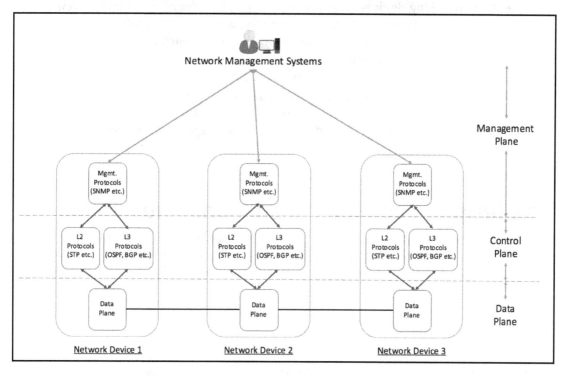

Figure 1: Networking planes.

Key aspects of the networking planes

In order to understand the driving factors behind SDN, it is important to understand some key aspects of the three planes of networking:

- Forwarding decisions are made locally within a networking device and those decisions are based on the *control plane*.
- The actual act of forwarding packets must be really fast, to meet the network performance requirements. This is implemented using specialized ASIC-based hardware, and implies that data plane entities exist on each physical networking device.

- Control plane learning involves more than one networking devices such as switches and routers for most common scenarios. It is comparatively much slower than the forwarding plane.
- All networking devices must support standard protocols in order for accurate learning of network topology, connectivity, and the related information. This in turn means that control plane entities must exist on each device.
- In multi-vendor situations, control plane and management plane inter-operability is crucial for smooth functioning of networks.
- Parts of management plane protocols such as SNMP are required to run on the networking devices. Nevertheless, the most critical aspect of management is the centralized functions provided by Network Management Systems (EMS and NMS).

Challenges faced by traditional networks

As seen earlier, traditional networks are built and operated based on the three networking planes. The networks were static in nature and were manually configured based on service requests. Let's now see what challenges are faced in the traditional architecture of networks.

Control plane challenges

The most obvious problem faced in control plane is that of interoperability. While standards exist for most protocols, each vendor's support for the standards may vary. And even for the same vendor the protocol behavior could differ between releases. This will lead to incompatibility and limit the intelligence that can be built using control plane. For cost optimization as well as flexibility, cloud operators do not want single-vendor lock in. Therefore, it is very important that the control plane is feature rich and robust for the entire cloud.

Another problem faced by control plane is that of scale. We have seen that control plane entities (protocols and so on) run on networking devices. These devices have limited compute resources, and for large-scale networks, the control plane processing may be hampered due to this. Traditional methods to scale the control plane were to either do a hardware upgrade of the full device or at least the control plane processor card on the network device. In cloud deployments, this will be a serious challenge, especially because applications and virtualized workloads are meant to scale up or down based on demand.

Management plane challenges

While the control plane has standard protocols that ensure basic interoperability, the management plane can be implemented with completely proprietary standards. Protocols such as SNMP are helpful, but for better user experience most vendors implement their own CLI and/or Element Management Systems (EMS). This makes the management of multi-vendor networks very cumbersome.

Cloud-based application deployment and the corresponding infrastructure need to be highly elastic. This means that resources need to be allocated and removed on demand. Cloud platforms such as OpenStack require the provisioning of resources to be available via programmatic APIs. This allows compute, storage, and networking resources to be allocated dynamically and optimally. Programmability in traditional networks was supported by automating CLI commands or via other north-bound interfaces. But due to the silo-based approach, it was difficult to integrate these APIs with compute and storage APIs.

Traditional applications required specialized networking hardware such as load balancers, firewalls, and so on. As applications became virtualized, it was imperative that specialized networking functions were also available in virtual form factor. This trend is commonly termed as **Network Function Virtualization** (**NFV**). This means that networking capabilities can be instantiated and deployed like software applications, independent of the actual hardware. In order to support this capability, cloud platforms require networks to be *defined using abstractions*. These abstractions allow entire applications and the related resources to be defined as software entities. And cloud platforms can *orchestrate* or *instantiate* these entities on demand.

SDN reference architecture

We have seen the traditional network architecture and the challenges faced by them. Let us now look at a typical SDN architecture and how it addresses these challenges.

The following diagram depicts a simplified SDN architecture where the control plane is centralized into a controller. It also considers OpenFlow as the protocol between the centralized control plane and the distributed data plane. While OpenFlow is the most popular SDN protocol between control and data plane, SDN platforms such as OpenContrail use XMPP and BGP as control plane protocols:

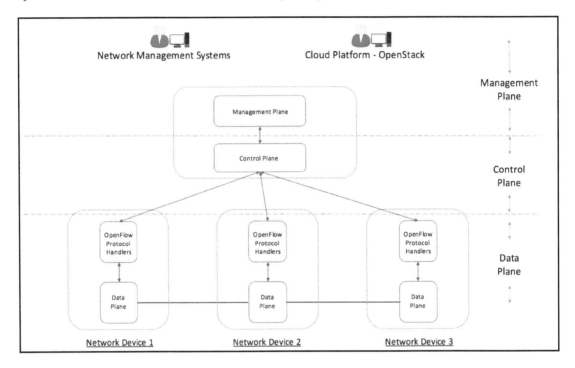

Figure 2: Simplified SDN-based network architecture.

Control plane improvements with SDN

In traditional networks, control plane was distributed and running on each networking device. The SDN model is to *centralize* the control plane. This centralized control plane is basically a software entity commonly referred to as the SDN controller. By centralizing the control plane, the interoperability problem is addressed to a large extent. The centralized control plane programs the device using technologies such as OpenFlow. All vendors who support protocols like OpenFlow can easily be integrated into SDN controllers. Furthermore, the data plane of new devices can be easily programmed since the control plane information base is readily available.

The problem of scale is also addressed more easily with a centralized controller. Most networking vendors run control plane entities on common off the shelf hardware. Similarly, a centralized controller is also designed to run on popular hardware platforms. In fact, it is also possible to run controllers as virtual machines. This allows the control plane to scale independently of the data plane scale and use cheap hardware.

Management plane improvements with SDN

Even with traditional network architecture, the management functionality was already centralized as network management systems. With the SDN architecture, there are added benefits where management plane interaction with control plane can be supported on the controller directly. This is very important when managing large networks and also multi-vendor networks.

Another benefit of centralized management and control planes is better modeling or abstraction of network functionality. Since management software now deals with a single centralized controller, we can support more robust programmatic interfaces since the complexity is hidden from the management plane. This results in the management plane exposing rich network abstractions that can be leveraged by cloud platforms such as OpenStack.

SDN and OpenStack

In order to understand how SDN fits into the OpenStack ecosystem, let's revisit some of the learnings from the earlier sections of this chapter:

- Network abstractions are required in order to provide a flexible environment for cloud-based applications
- Networking must support programmatic APIs in order to dynamically provision the resources needed for applications and to integrate effectively with compute and storage resources
- Centralized management of SDN is critical to support multi-vendor based cloud infrastructure

OpenStack and Network abstractions

As seen in the previous chapter, OpenStack supports simple abstractions such as network, subnet, router, firewall, and so on. These abstractions help cloud users to *define* applications and the required infrastructure as software entities. The advantage of this approach is that underlying physical infrastructure is unaware and independent of the applications running on it. Sophisticated orchestration entities and SDN controllers can be leveraged to *instantiate* the applications and networking resources on demand. It is clear that OpenStack abstractions for networking integrate very smoothly with the SDN architecture.

OpenStack and RESTful API

One of the management challenges for traditional networking was lack of well-known APIs to program the network. Without these APIs, it is difficult to provide flexible, on-demand infrastructure. OpenStack was designed from the ground up to support RESTful APIs using HTTP for each and every component. This provides powerful management and integration capabilities. In addition, cloud vendors can easily enhance and supplement the capabilities by leveraging these APIs.

OpenStack and centralized management

OpenStack supports web-based management as well as the CLI. These tools use the RESTful APIs supported by various OpenStack components. SDN architecture benefits of better abstractions and programmatic API for networking and in powerful centralized management capability using OpenStack. End users can provision compute, storage, and networking resources with ease and flexibility, thereby providing their applications with the best possible resources.

Summary

This chapter highlighted the architecture and components of traditional networks. With the increasing adoption of scalable and dynamic applications, the control plane, and management plane design of traditional networks faced challenges. SDN is a new approach where most of the control plane software is centralized into an SDN controller. This also helps provide better management which was already centralized. Finally, we looked at how the benefits of SDN can be easily realized in OpenStack-based cloud deployment. In the next two chapters, we will look into the control plane and the data plane aspects of SDN with specific focus on Open vSwitch-based networking.

3
SDN Protocols

In the previous chapter, we outlined the challenges of traditional networks and showed how a SDN architecture with its distributed control plane and centralized management offers a superior solution. In this chapter, we will delve into the underlying components and protocols that enable the SDN-based architecture. We will introduce **Open vSwitch** (**OVS**), a popular virtual switch in SDN environments and leverage it to gain insights into SDN building blocks.

We will cover the following topics in this chapter:

- How protocols with definition of standard API are the key driver for the SDN architecture and solutions.
- Introduction to Open vSwitch
- Data modeling language: YANG (RFC 6020), data model: YANG data models, Encoding formats: XML, JSON, and YAML
- Protocols: OpenFlow, NETCONF, RESTCONF, OF-CONFIG, OVSDB, and their role in SDN eco-system
- Learning the protocols using sample configurations of software that implement and tools supporting configuration, monitoring of the packet flow

Getting familiar with SDN protocols

In pre-SDN architectures, although there is a separation between the control plane and the data plane, the communication between the layers is usually proprietary and it is defined by the *merchant* silicon vendor or network equipment vendors. Moreover, the network management configuration syntax is not interoperable between networking gear from different vendors, for instance, CLI for Cisco IOS is not compatible with Juniper's JUNOS CLI.

The definition of standard protocols with open APIs between control plane and data plane in addition to a standardized configuration model is the catalyst that is enabling the SDN. This standard API-based separation of the control plane from the forwarding plane enables consistent management and control across network. It also facilitates interoperability between forwarding planes and control planes between networking equipment from different vendors. The ability to communicate with forwarding elements across the network through centralized control plane protocols facilitates use cases such as network-wide custom traffic engineering, besides providing a network-wide operational view for ease of manageability.

In this chapter, we will use OVS with a rich set of utilities as a platform to understand the SDN paradigm with hands-on configuration samples in a Linux environment. It is important to note that OVS is the most widely used virtual switch in OpenStack environments.

Open vSwitch

Let's start with an introduction to OVS, a production quality, multilayer virtual switch popularly deployed in virtualized environments. Open vSwitch is licensed under the open source Apache 2.0 license, and is included as default feature from Linux 3.3 Kernel onwards.

In addition to bringing in L2 learning, L3 forwarding, and ACL features that are typically found in switching processors, OVS supports features tailored for virtualized deployments. OVS supports fine-grained Quality of Service (QoS), control across traffic aggregate connections, and per VM interface traffic policing. OVS also supports visibility into inter-VM communication via NetFlow, sFlow(R), IPFIX, SPAN, RSPAN, and GRE-tunneled mirrors. It supports tunneling protocols popular in virtualized environments such as GRE, VXLAN, STT, and Geneve, with IPsec.

OVS supports mobility of state by live network state reconstruction of virtual machines as they migrate between different hosts. It supports remote triggers for the changes in the network dynamics. Open vSwitch supports methods to append and manipulate tags in the network packets that uniquely identify a VM in a network context

OVS supports OpenFlow protocols including many virtualization extensions. The following diagram describes the OVS components and interaction between them:

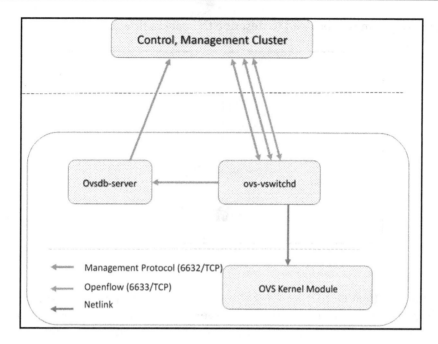

Figure 1: Open vSwitch components.

Open vSwitch's modular architecture with switching daemons (**ovs-vswitchd**) and sets of software utilities allows its deployment as the control stack for switching silicon. With Linux kernel module (`openvswitch_mod.ko`) for flow-based switching, OVS functions as soft switch running within the hypervisor.

ovs-vswitchd communicates with OpenFlow controller using OpenFlow. It communicates with **Ovsdb-server** using OVSDB protocol. It communicates with the kernel module over netlink, and with the system through the netdev abstract interface.

ovs-vswitchd (slow path) implements core switching features, including learning VLAN and bonding via programming the flow table, which is also exposed via OpenFlow. It supports visibility via NetFlow, sFlow(R), IPFIX, SPAN, RSPAN, and GRE-tunneled mirrors. The packet classifier supports lookup based on L2-L4 wildcarding, priorities and actions to forward, drop, and modify packets. It monitors the data-path flow counters to handle flow expiration.

ovs-vswitchd supports centralized control, having one OpenFlow connection per OpenFlow Logical Switch. It exports an idealized view of OpenFlow Logical Switch. Queue missed flows go to the central controller.

The following diagram will be used to describe the packet flow in the OVS:

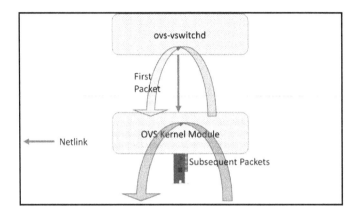

Figure 2: Open vSwitch packet flow.

The Kernel module (fast path) `openvswitch_mod.ko` handles packet lookup, switching, and tunneling efficiently. It caches flows; however, it does not have OpenFlow awareness. It extracts the packet header and generates the hash to use it as an index to find a match in the flow table. If a flow match is found, it performs actions to modify, forward, and tunnel encapsulate/de-capsulate as programed by the controller and increments packet counters. If there is no flow entry, the packet is sent to **ovs-vswitchd** and eventually to the controller if configured. **ovs-vswitchd**, in consultation with the controller takes decision on how to process the packet and programs the data path's actions for the flow. Once the flow is programmed with the actions, the subsequent packets are handled in the kernel fast path based on the flow match and actions.

OVS provides a rich set of command-line utilities supporting configuration, monitoring, and debugging:

- `ovs-vsctl`: This command-line utility configures `ovs-vswitchd` interfacing with its configuration database; it connects to an `ovsdb-server` process that maintains an Open vSwitch configuration database. It provides interface to push the commands and waits for `ovs-vswitchd` to finish reconfiguring. It supports commands to create Open vSwitch bridges, configure ports, interfaces, and setting up the OpenFlow controller.
- `ovs-ofctl`: This command-line tool is for monitoring and administering OpenFlow switches. It can also show the current state of an OpenFlow switch, including features, configuration, and OpenFlow table entries.

- `ovs-appctl`: This program provides a way to invoke the commands supported by Open vSwitch daemons, `ovs-vswitchd`. `ovs-appctl` sends the command and prints the daemon's response on a standard output.
- `ovs-dpctl`: This program can create, modify, and delete Open vSwitch datapaths that are implemented outside of `ovs-vswitchd`, such as the Linux kernel-based datapaths.

Configuration management protocols

The configuration management protocols such as SNMP lack support for features required for SDN deployments. Transactions across multiple network elements, the ability to back up and restore configuration, error recovery, and operational ease are vital for large scale SDN deployments.

SDN implementations define sets of protocols that support programming the control plane and switching configuration management. Protocols are designed for extensibility, interoperability, and reuse of configuration components to fit into SDN deployment requirements. Protocols can be classified based on their role.

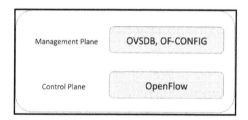

Figure 3: SDN Protocol Classification.

Control plane protocols such as the OpenFlow program the forwarding path, while configuration management protocols such as **OVSDB**, and NETCONF-based **OF-CONFIG** are network configuration protocols used for configuring networking equipment, performing switching and routing.

For instance, an action to bring up the interface, creating a tunnel is programmed by **OF-CONFIG/OVSDB**, while programming packet flow in the networking device is performed by OpenFlow.

Protocols

Data models define the structure, syntax, and semantics of the data encoded, while the encoding formats define the format for encoding data providing a flexible human-readable representation.

Let us start by reviewing the YANG (RFC 6020) data modeling language and YANG data models.

YANG

RFC 6020 defines YANG as follows:

> *"YANG is a data modeling language used to model configuration and state data manipulated by the Network Configuration Protocol (NETCONF), NETCONF remote procedure calls, and NETCONF notifications."*

YANG data models define structure, syntax, and semantics of encoded data. NETCONF defines primitives to encode, view, and manipulate the data. YANG presents human readable format of XML data that NETCONF acts on. It structures the data into a hierarchical tree leaf node representation and provides a separation of configuration data and state data. It also defines a format to place constraints on the data and framework for extensions to base.

The YANG module contains header information, includes, imports, element data type definitions, configuration, state data declaration, notification subscriptions, and RPC actions.

YIN

XML representation of YANG is defined as **YANG Independent Notation (YIN)**. YIN converts YANG statements to XML, preserving the structure and content of YANG. Conversion is loss-less and reversible, maintaining complete semantic equivalence. Converting YANG statements to XML enables use of off-the-shelf XML parsers eliminating the need for the YANG parser.

pyang

pyang is a Python program to validate YANG modules (RFC 6020). It is also used to convert YANG modules into equivalent YIN modules. You can refer to the online documentation at `https://github.com/mbj4668/pyang/wiki/Documentation`.

1. To install `pyang` you can use the `pip` command:

   `$ sudo pip install pyang`

2. Use the `tree` plugin of `pyang` to get an overview of the data model schemas as follows:

```
root@openstack-base:~/pyang/doc/tutorial/examples# pyang -f tree turing-machine.yang
module: turing-machine
   +--rw turing-machine
      +--ro state                state-index
      +--ro head-position        cell-index
      +--ro tape
      |  +--ro cell* [coord]
      |     +--ro coord    cell-index
      |     +--ro symbol?  tape-symbol
      +--rw transition-function
         +--rw delta* [label]
            +--rw label      string
            +--rw input
            |  +--rw state    state-index
            |  +--rw symbol   tape-symbol
            +--rw output
               +--rw state?      state-index
               +--rw symbol?     tape-symbol
               +--rw head-move?  head-dir
rpcs:
   +---x initialize
   |  +---w input
   |     +---w tape-content?   string
   +---x run
notifications:
   +---n halted
      +--ro state    state-index
```

3. You can also view the contents of the `yang` file. For example, `turning-machine.yang`:

```
module turing-machine {

  namespace "http://example.net/turing-machine";

  prefix "tm";

  description
    "Data model for the Turing Machine.";

  revision 2013-12-27 {
    description
      "Initial revision.";
  }

  /* Typedefs */

  typedef tape-symbol {
    type string {
      length "0..1";
    }
    description
      "Type of symbols appearing in tape cells.

       A blank is represented as an empty string where necessary.";
  }
```

4. You can also convert the YANG file into YIN:

```
$ pyang turning-machine.yang -f yin
```

```xml
<?xml version="1.0" encoding="UTF-8"?>
<module name="turing-machine"
        xmlns="urn:ietf:params:xml:ns:yang:yin:1"
        xmlns:tm="http://example.net/turing-machine">
  <namespace uri="http://example.net/turing-machine"/>
  <prefix value="tm"/>
  <description>
    <text>Data model for the Turing Machine.</text>
  </description>
  <revision date="2013-12-27">
    <description>
      <text>Initial revision.</text>
    </description>
  </revision>
  <typedef name="tape-symbol">
    <type name="string">
      <length value="0..1"/>
    </type>
    <description>
      <text>Type of symbols appearing in tape cells.

A blank is represented as an empty string where necessary.</text>
    </description>
```

NETCONF

NETCONF (RFC 6241) defines an XML-based **remote procedure call** (**RPC**) mechanism for installing, manipulating, and deleting configuration of network devices. Drawing conceptually from Juniper's XML encoded RPC-based JunosScript, NETCONF is designed to be a network operator and **DevOps** friendly with low implementation and maintenance costs. NETCONF operates at the configuration and management layer of the network.

NETCONF supports the distinction between configuration data and data on operational status of the device, the ability to save and restore the device's configuration data, and compares configuration data across multiple devices. It supports transactions-based configuration and model-based network wide configuration across multiple devices. Transaction models ensure atomicity, consistency, independency, and durability of the configuration data. It supports delayed orchestration of the configuration data to the device, delayed service activation, testing and rejecting configuration, and the rollback of configuration to previous versions.

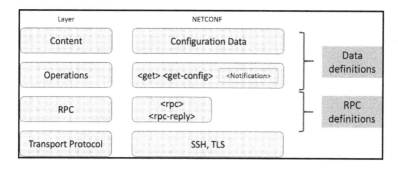

Figure 4: NETCONF protocol layers.

The NETCONF protocol defines layered architectures consisting of the following layers:

- **Content layer**: Device configuration and notification data store.
- **Operations layer**: Set of operations to manipulate configuration data in the data store.
- **RPC Messages layer**: Supports remote procedure calls (RPCs) and notifications.
- **Secure Transport layer**: TCP-based secure transport protocol for reliable transport of messages. **Specifies Secure Shell (SSH)** as the mandatory option and TLS as an alternative option.

NETCONF provides mechanisms to extend capabilities beyond the base specification defined in RFC 6241 (Writable-Running*, Candidate configuration*, Confirmed Commit, Rollback-on-Error, Validate, Distinct Startup*, and URL and XPath capabilities). NETCONF Manager (client) initiates connection with the NETCONF server (device) with a `<hello>` message indicating client capabilities. The server responds with a `<hello>` message containing device capabilities. This message exchange baselines that support at both ends; it also acts as a mechanism to extend beyond base capabilities and modify current capabilities.

RFC 5277 defines NETCONF event notifications, providing an asynchronous message delivery mechanism. The NETCONF client initiates a subscription to receive event notifications, and the NETCONF server responds to subscription requests. If the request is successful, the server announces an event occurrence to the clients subscribing to the event.

Netopeer

Netopeer is a set of NETCONF tools built on the `libnetconf` library. It supports communication with NETCONF-enabled devices. The `netopeer-cli` is an open source implementation of the NETCONF client. It supports client operations defined by the protocol: `https://trac.tools.ietf.org/wg/netconf/trac/wiki`.

The following link has some instructions to install `netopeer-cli` from the source: `https://github.com/CESNET/netopeer`.

The following command lists the features supported by the `netopeer-cli` client:

```
netconf> help
Netopeer CLI client, version 0.8.0
built from git a5bdc48a674e9bfa2ca3
compile time: Jul  7 2016, 22:56:20

 Available commands:
 help            Display this text
 connect         Connect to a NETCONF server
 listen          Listen for a NETCONF Call Home
 disconnect      Disconnect from a NETCONF server
 commit          NETCONF <commit> operation
 copy-config     NETCONF <copy-config> operation
 delete-config   NETCONF <delete-config> operation
 discard-changes NETCONF <discard-changes> operation
 edit-config     NETCONF <edit-config> operation
 get             NETCONF <get> operation
 get-config      NETCONF <get-config> operation
 get-schema      NETCONF <get-schema> operation
 kill-session    NETCONF <kill-session> operation
 lock            NETCONF <lock> operation
 unlock          NETCONF <unlock> operation
 validate        NETCONF <validate> operation
 test            Run a specified test case
 subscribe       NETCONF Event Notifications <create-subscription> operation
 time            Enable/disable measuring time of command execution
 knownhosts      Manage known hosts in the "~/.ssh/known_hosts" file
 status          Print information about the current NETCONF session
 user-rpc        Send your own content in an RPC envelope (for DEBUG purposes)
 verbose         Enable/disable verbose messages
 quit            Quit the program
 auth            Manage SSH authentication options
 capability      Add/remove capability to/from the list of supported capabilities
 editor          Manage the editor to be used for manual XML pasting/writing

 To delete a command history entry, use CTRL+X.
```

Figure 4: Netconf CLI client.

The `netopeer` client allows users to establish a session with the NETCONF server running in the devices supporting it. It provides commands to connect, validate the `netconf` operations, and perform configuration changes. It supports sending the NETCONF Remote Procedure Call (RPC) subscribing to the NETCON event notifications.

OF-CONFIG

Open Networking Foundation is defines the **OF-CONFIG** protocol to manage the configuration operation of an **OpenFlow Switch**. OF-CONFIG 1.2 leverages the NETCONF protocol as the transport protocol. OF-CONFIG 1.2 defines the XML schema for the content layer of the NETCONF protocol and companion YANG module for the **OF-CONFIG** data model. OF-CONFIG 1.2 defines the XML schema normative constraints that the YANG module conforms to:

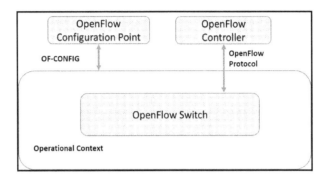

Figure 5: The OF-CONFIG architecture.

Developed as a complementary protocol to the **OpenFlow Switch** specification (**OF-SWITCH**), OF-CONFIG 1.2 is focused on functions required to configure an OpenFlow 1.3 logical switch. An OpenFlow Logical Switch is an instantiation of an **OpenFlow Switch** with a set of resources (example ports), which can be associated with an OpenFlow controller.

It supports OpenFlow controller assignments to OpenFlow data planes. It also supports configuration of ports, queues, tunnel types such as IP-in-GRE, NV-GRE, VxLAN, modification of operational status such as ports, capability discovery of the OpenFlow logical switch, instantiation of OpenFlow Logical Switches (OpenFlow datapaths), and certificate configuration for secure communication.

OF-CONFIG 1.2 defines an extensible framework laying the foundation for advanced configuration support.

OVSDB

Open vSwitch Database (OVSDB) is a switch configuration management protocol. Originally part of OVS, the OVSDB protocol is now Informational RFC(`https://tools.iet f.org/html/rfc7047`).

OVSDB provides a complementary functionality to OpenFlow, similar to NETCONF /OF-CONF. OVSDB supports operations to create, read, update, and delete OpenFlow datapaths (bridges), tunnel interfaces, ports, queues, QoS configuration, configuring controllers for OpenFlow datapath, managers for OVSDB servers, and statistics collection.

JSON-RPC transport

Based on JSON-RPC 1.0, OVSDB specifies a JSON-RPC object consisting of `method`, `params`, and `id`. The `method` property contains the name of the method to invoke the `params` points to an array of objects passed as method arguments and `id` is the request-ID that is used to match the response-ID.

Key methods include `transact`, the RPC method used by the OVSDB client to update the configuration database on an OVSDB server and the `monitor` method that subscribes a client to receive notifications whenever any of the listed tables/columns receive any changes. This mechanism is useful to notify OVSDB clients of changes to OVSDB for taking appropriate actions. The `update` notification is used by the server to notify clients that have requested a `monitor` of changes in the tables:

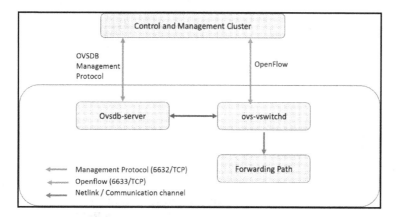

Figure 6: OVSDB Architecture.

OVS packages **Ovsdb-server** that provides RPC interfaces to an OVSDB. It supports JSON-RPC client connections over active or passive TCP/IP or Unix domain sockets. It can accept configuration information from an interactive OVSDB client, `ovsdb-client`. This OVSDB client can also be with a controller platform like OpenDaylight. **ovs-vswitchd** is a daemon that manages and controls Open vSwitch switches. `ovs-vswitchd` connects to **Ovsdb-server** from `unix:/var/run/openvswitch/db.sock` by default.

You can install OVS using the following command on Ubuntu-based servers:

```
$ sudo apt-get install openvswitch
```

`Open_vSwitch` is the default OVS database for Open vSwitch:

```
# ovsdb-client  list-dbs
Open_vSwitch
```

The following command shows the trace of the JSON RPC command edited for brevity:

```
# ovs-vsctl -vjsonrpc show
jsonrpc|DBG|unix:/var/run/openvswitch/db.sock:
send request, method="monitor", params=["Open_vSwitch",null,{"Port":{"columns":
["interfaces","name","tag","trunks"]},"Interface":{"columns":["error","name","options","type"]},"Controller":{"columns":
["is_connected","target"]},"Manager":{"columns":["is_connected","target"]},"Bridge":{"columns":
["controller","fail_mode","name","ports"]},"Open_vSwitch":{"columns":
["bridges","cur_cfg","manager_options","ovs_version"]}}], id=1

|jsonrpc|DBG|unix:/var/run/openvswitch/db.sock:
received reply, result={"Interface":{"15a9a2b4-bb27-4f3c-9071-85b6b1fc783d":{"new":{"name":"ofc-bridge","options":
["map",[]],"error":["set",[]],"type":"internal"}}},"Port":{"92f78b90-7040-4a53-8e8e-dd536d4ef73e":{"new":{"name":"ofc-
bridge","interfaces": ["uuid","15a9a2b4-bb27-4f3c-9071-85b6b1fc783d"], "trunks":["set",[]], "tag":["set",[]]}}},
"Bridge":{"29bf05d3-2304-4e8e-b09d-a29256c10399":    {"new":{"name":"ofc-bridge","ports":
["uuid","92f78b90-7040-4a53-8e8e-dd536d4ef73e"],    "fail_mode":"secure","controller":["set",[]]}}}, "Open_vSwitch":
{"927a70da-6295-4d15-b62a 7ba83ec96fc9":{"new":{"manager_options": ["set",[]],"bridges":["uuid","29bf05d3-2304-4e8e-
b09d-a29256c10399"], "cur_cfg":0,"ovs_version":["set",[]]}}}}, id=1

927a70da-6295-4d15-b62a-7ba83ec96fc9
    Bridge ofc-bridge
        fail_mode: secure
        Port ofc-bridge
            Interface ofc-bridge
                type: internal
```

OVSDB schema

OVSDB consists of a set of tables with a database schema or blueprint defined in the OVSDB schema document: `http://openvswitch.org/ovs-vswitchd.conf.db.5.pdf`. The following diagram shows the relationship among most commonly used tables in the OVSDB. **Open_vSwitch** is the root table, along with tables for **Bridge**, **Port**, and **Interface**:

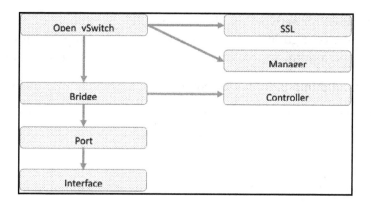

Figure 7: OVSDB flow tables.

The **Open vSwitch** system on any given server can support multiple layer 2 bridges. And each bridge can have more than one port. A port is most commonly associated with only one interface. However, it is possible to use a bond and associate more than one interface to an OVS **Port**. This is quite similar to physical network interfaces. The Bridge, Port, and Interface tables reflect the data path entities.

The **Manager**, **Controller**, and **SSL** interfaces are the management and control plane related tables with OVSDB. Each bridge can be associated with one or more **Controller**. Managers refer to the OVSDB clients that a given OVS system must communicate with and exchange configuration information.

The `ovsdb-client` dump command lists the following tables:

```
root@openstack-base:~# ovsdb-client list-tables
Table
------------------------
Port
Manager
Bridge
Interface
SSL
IPFIX
Open_vSwitch
Queue
NetFlow
Controller
QoS
Mirror
Flow_Sample_Collector_Set
sFlow
Flow_Table
```

OVSDB contains tables for network entities such as `Port`, `Bridge`, and `Interface`. It has `Flow Table` for flow configuration. It has a database for sampling features such as `NetFlow`, `sFlow`, and a mirroring feature. It supports databases for `Queue` and `QoS`.

The `ovsdb` command dump indicates the columns list for the `Bridge`, as follows:

```
root@openstack-base:~# ovsdb-client list-columns Bridge
Column              Type
------------------  --------------------------------------------------------------------------------
------------------------
name                "string"
flood_vlans         {"key":{"maxInteger":4095,"minInteger":0,"type":"integer"},"max":4096,"min":0}
stp_enable          "boolean"
auto_attach         {"key":{"refTable":"AutoAttach","type":"uuid"},"min":0}
ports               {"key":{"refTable":"Port","type":"uuid"},"max":"unlimited","min":0}
rstp_enable         "boolean"
_uuid               "uuid"
fail_mode           {"key":{"enum":["set",["secure","standalone"]],"type":"string"},"min":0}
rstp_status         {"key":"string","max":"unlimited","min":0,"value":"string"}
flow_tables         {"key":{"maxInteger":254,"minInteger":0,"type":"integer"},"max":"unlimited","min":0,"value":
{"refTable":"Flow_Table","type":"uuid"}}
_version            "uuid"
netflow             {"key":{"refTable":"NetFlow","type":"uuid"},"min":0}
controller          {"key":{"refTable":"Controller","type":"uuid"},"max":"unlimited","min":0}
datapath_type       "string"
external_ids        {"key":"string","max":"unlimited","min":0,"value":"string"}
other_config        {"key":"string","max":"unlimited","min":0,"value":"string"}
ipfix               {"key":{"refTable":"IPFIX","type":"uuid"},"min":0}
status              {"key":"string","max":"unlimited","min":0,"value":"string"}
datapath_id         {"key":"string","min":0}
mirrors             {"key":{"refTable":"Mirror","type":"uuid"},"max":"unlimited","min":0}
mcast_snooping_enable "boolean"
datapath_version    "string"
protocols           {"key":{"enum":["set",
["OpenFlow10","OpenFlow11","OpenFlow12","OpenFlow13","OpenFlow14","OpenFlow15"]],"type":"string"},"max":"unlimited","min":0}
sflow               {"key":{"refTable":"sFlow","type":"uuid"},"min":0}
```

OF-CONFIG server for Open vSwitch

OVS implements its own Open vSwitch Database management (OVSDB) protocol for switch configuration management. **OF-CONFIG Server** for OVS is a migration path to ONF standards based on OF-CONFIG:

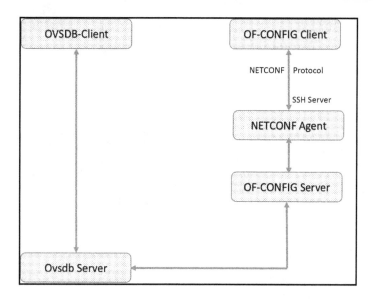

Figure 8: OF-CONFIG architecture.

OF-CONFIG Server in OVS is a glue layer presenting a NETCONF-based interface OF-CONFIG interface to **OF-CONFIG Client** while interfacing with the **Ovsdb Server**. This design ensures that the tight coupling of the **Ovsdb Server** in the OVS architecture is retained.

Implementation consists of the `ofc-agent` and `ofc-server` applications derived from the `netopeer` project with an underlying `libnetconf` library supporting the `netconf` protocol. The communication between the `ofc-agent` and `ofc-server` is implemented using D-Bus (by default) or the UNIX socket. It connects to the OVSDB using OVSDB IDL.

Follow the instructions at `https://github.com/openvswitch/of-config/blob/master/INSTALL.md` to build an OF-CONFIG server, `ofc-server`.

Let's see how the NETCONF client, `netopeer-cli`, communicates with the OF-CONFIG server `ofc-server` to access the OVSDB:

1. Start `ofc-server`:

```
$ ofc-server -v 3 -f -d unix://var/run/openvswitch/db.sock
ofc-server[10304]: Try to synchronize OVSDB.
2016-09-25T05:49:46Z|00001|reconnect|INFO|unix://var/run/openvswitch/db.sock: connecting...
2016-09-25T05:49:46Z|00002|reconnect|INFO|unix://var/run/openvswitch/db.sock: connected
ofc-server[10304]: OF-CONFIG datastore initialized.
ofc-server[10304]: Datastore of-config initiated with ID 846930887.
ofc-server[10304]: Setting default configuration for ietf-netconf-server module
ofc-server[10304]: callback_srv_netconf_srv_ssh_srv_listen_oneport: port 830
ofc-server[10304]: callback_srv_netconf_srv_ssh_srv_listen: started sshd (PID 10310)
ofc-server[10304]: OFC COPY-CONFIG (from <config> to running)
ofc-server[10304]: Deleting all OVSDB content
ofc-server[10304]: OVSDB transaction successful
ofc-server[10304]: OVSDB unchanged
ofc-server[10304]: OFC COPY-CONFIG (from startup to running)
ofc-server[10304]: Creating the node capable-switch
ofc-server[10304]: Creating the node id
ofc-server[10304]: Creating the node resources
ofc-server[10304]: Creating the node port
ofc-server[10304]: Creating the node logical-switches
ofc-server[10304]: Creating the node switch
ofc-server[10304]: OVSDB transaction successful
```

2. Use a NETCONF client such as `netopeer-cli` to connect to `ofc-server` for configuration and data queries:

```
netconf> connect --login sreeniv 127.0.0.1
sreeniv@127.0.0.1 password:
```

3. Issue the `get-config` command from `netopeer-cli`:

```
netconf> get-config

Select target datastore (running|startup|candidate|url:<dsturl>): running
```

4. `ofc-server` receives the NETCONF request and responds with an update:

```
ofc-server[10304]: Some message received
ofc-server[10304]: Processing request <?xml version="1.0" encoding="UTF-8"?>
<rpc xmlns="urn:ietf:params:xml:ns:netconf:base:1.0" message-id="1">
  <get-config>
    <source>
      <running/>
    </source>
  </get-config>
</rpc>
ofc-server[10304]: OpenFlow: connecting to unix://var/run/openvswitch/ofc-bridge.mgmt
....
....
ofc-server[10304]: OpenFlow: ofc-bridge: successful connection.
```

5. The update is reflected on the `netopeer-cli` console:

```
Result:
<capable-switch xmlns="urn:onf:config:yang">
    <id>openvswitch</id>
    <resources>
      <port>
        <name>ofc-bridge</name>
        <requested-number>666</requested-number>
        <configuration>
          <admin-state>down</admin-state>
          <no-receive>false</no-receive>
          <no-forward>false</no-forward>
          <no-packet-in>false</no-packet-in>
        </configuration>
      </port>
    </resources>
    <logical-switches>
      <switch>
        <id>ofc-bridge</id>
        <datapath-id>00:01:02:03:04:05:06:07</datapath-id>
        <lost-connection-behavior>failSecureMode</lost-connection-behavior>
        <resources>
          <port>ofc-bridge</port>
        </resources>
      </switch>
    </logical-switches>
  </capable-switch>
```

6. Check the output from the `ovs-vsctl` command to verify that the `datapath_id` matches with that of the `of-server` response:

```
# ovs-vsctl list Bridge
_uuid                  : 29bf05d3-2304-4e8e-b09d-a29256c10399
auto_attach            : []
controller             : []
datapath_id            : "0001020304050607"
datapath_type          : ""
datapath_version       : "<unknown>"
external_ids           : {}
fail_mode              : secure
flood_vlans            : []
flow_tables            : {}
ipfix                  : []
mcast_snooping_enable: false
mirrors                : []
name                   : ofc-bridge
netflow                : []
other_config           : {datapath-id="0001020304050607"}
ports                  : [92f78b90-7040-4a53-8e8e-dd536d4ef73e]
protocols              : []
rstp_enable            : false
rstp_status            : {}
sflow                  : []
status                 : {}
stp_enable             : false
```

Understanding OpenFlow

The OpenFlow protocol is a key enabler in driving SDN solutions. OpenFlow is a standard protocol between data and control for remotely controlling the flow table of a switch or router:

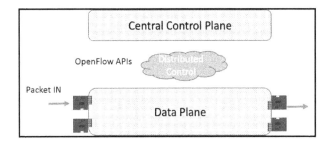

Figure 9: OpenFlow block diagram.

OpenFlow enables SDN controllers to define the flow of network packets across the network of devices supporting the OpenFlow protocol. OpenFlow defines a generalized flow table with a very flexible and generalized flow abstraction, Open control API, which enables remote control of layers1-7.

OpenFlow defines APIs for defining traffic flow and a framework for describing the flow state; hence, it can be viewed as the following.

OpenFlow as an API

OpenFlow is an outline semantic for defining flow characteristics of traffic and actions to take on the packets matching the defined characteristics.

OpenFlow as a control plane

OpenFlow provides a framework to define flow information and RPCs for a central SDN controller to program the flow state information. The state is maintained within an OpenFlow agent running on the forwarding network device.

OpenFlow tables

OpenFlow tables form a pipeline to accomplish packet header processing. The pipeline can be formed by a single flow table at the very least. Multiple flow tables form a pipeline, acting on input from previous flow tables:

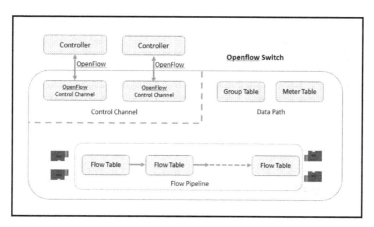

Figure 10: OpenFlow tables.

Let's refer to the dump of the Open vSwitch implementing OpenFlow version 1.4 to gain insight into the OpenFlow pipeline processing.

Check for the OpenFlow version:

```
# ovs-ofctl --version
ovs-ofctl (Open vSwitch) 2.5.0
Compiled Mar 10 2016 14:15:42
OpenFlow versions 0x1:0x4
```

OpenFlow matching

Packets hit `table 0 ("classifier")` at the start. The classifier matches the flow table entry for packet header parameters such as tunnel header, Ethernet, VLAN, MPLS, IPv4/IPv6, ARP, TCP/UDP, and ICMP to execute the instruction set included in the flow entry:

```
# ovs-ofctl  dump-table-features ofc-bridge
ovs-ofctl: dump-table-features needs OpenFlow 1.3 or later ('-O OpenFlow13')
root@openstack-base:~# ovs-ofctl  dump-table-features ofc-bridge -O OpenFlow13
  table 0 ("classifier"):
    metadata: match=0xffffffffffffffff write=0xffffffffffffffff
    max_entries=1000000
    instructions (table miss and others):
      next tables: 1-253
      instructions: meter,apply_actions,clear_actions,write_actions,write_metadata,goto_table
      Write-Actions and Apply-Actions features:
    matching:
      dp_hash: arbitrary mask
      recirc_id: exact match or wildcard
      conj_id: exact match or wildcard
      tun_id: arbitrary mask
      tun_src: arbitrary mask
      tun_dst: arbitrary mask
      tun_ipv6_src: arbitrary mask
      tun_ipv6_dst: arbitrary mask
      tun_flags: arbitrary mask
      tun_gbp_id: arbitrary mask
      tun_gbp_flags: arbitrary mask
      tun_metadata0: arbitrary mask
      metadata: arbitrary mask
      in_port: exact match or wildcard
      in_port_oxm: exact match or wildcard
      actset_output: exact match or wildcard
      pkt_mark: arbitrary mask
      ct_state: arbitrary mask
      ct_zone: exact match or wildcard
      ct_mark: arbitrary mask
      ct_label: arbitrary mask
```

If the instructions results in a packet header rewrite, the subsequent tables in the pipeline match the changed packet header. The significance of the match and action instructions is local to the flow table and the pipeline:

```
table 1 ("table1"):
  metadata: match=0xffffffffffffffff write=0xffffffffffffffff
  max_entries=1000000
  instructions (table miss and others):
    next tables: 2-253
    (same instructions)
    (same actions)
  |  (same matching)

  #
```

OpenFlow actions and instructions

The instructions field specifies a set of actions or modifications to the pipeline processing. The Open vSwitch instructions include meter, apply_actions, clear_actions, write_actions, write_metadata, and goto_table.

A flow entry can modify the action set using a write_actions instruction or a clear_actions instruction associated with a particular match. The action set is carried between flow tables.

The goto_table instruction setting indicates the next flow table in the pipeline. The next tables field in the tables defines the range for the goto_table, ensuring that the next table in the pipeline has an ID greater than its own ID. This instruction must be supported in all flow tables except the last one. The pipeline processing stops when the instruction set of a flow entry does not contain a goto_table instruction and the actions in the action set of the packet are executed.

OpenFlow specification (OFv1.5) can be described as follows:

Name	Description and use
match fields	Matches packets such as tunnel header, Ethernet, VLAN, MPLS, IPv4/IPv6, ARP, TCP/UDP, port number, and optionally information from a previous table if there is more than one.
priority	Matching precedence. The `match` field combined with the `priority` field is used to identify the table entry and must be unique.
counters	Keeps track of the number of times the flow has been matched.
instructions	Defines sets of `actionsmeter`, `apply_actions`, `clear_actions`, `write_actions`, and `write_metadata`. `goto_table` modifies the pipeline processing.
timeouts	Used to control how long until a flow is removed from the switch.
cookie	A value used by the controller to help identify a flow, for example, when filtering requests. Not used in packet processing.
flags	Used to manage flow entries.

OpenFlow Wireshark Dissector

Install Wireshark in Ubuntu:

```
% sudo apt-get install wireshark
```

The following screenshot depicts a Wireshark capture of the OpenFlow packets. The packet frame shows `Match` on MAC `46:1c:69:c8:b9:77` and `Action` to `output` on `Port 1`:

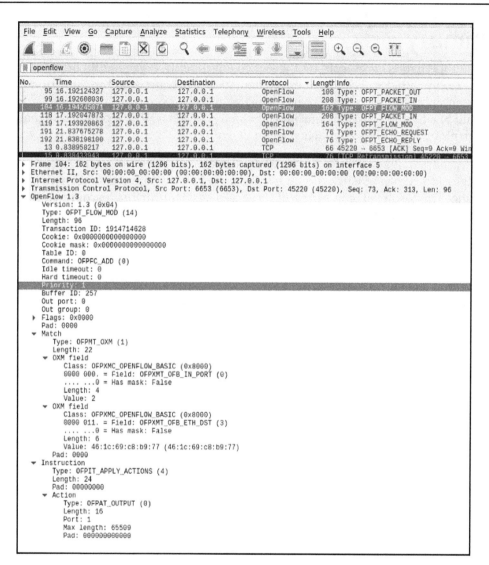

Figure 11: Wireshark dump of OpenFlow with Match and Action.

Summary

As seen in this chapter, protocols are the key enablers of SDN. We highlighted some key protocols along with details on their implementation. We touched upon data modeling language and encoding formats. We have also seen how various protocols fit together for an end-to-end SDN solution. We've introduced Open vSwitch (OVS), a popular virtual switch in SDN deployments. We also touched upon OpenFlow internals.

In the next chapter, we will build on the understanding of OpenFlow, and leverage the knowledge of the Open vSwitch toolkit to dive deep into the internals of OpenFlow-based networking. This knowledge in turn will serve as a basis for further learning on the internals of OpenStack networking.

4

SDN Networking with Open vSwitch

In Chapter 3, *SDN Protocols*, we learned about the key protocols enabling SDN-based solutions and Open vSwitch implementation of OpenFlow. In this chapter, we will build on the knowledge to gain insights into how these components fit together to implement SDN networking. We will begin with lightweight virtual networking with a Linux network namespace and Open vSwitch functioning as a conventional L2 switch. We will then bring OpenFlow into the mix to depict the flow-based networking with virtual machines, interfacing with SDN Controller. We will introduce Mininet, a network emulation tool for prototyping network topologies. Finally, we will depict the architecture of Neutron, the networking component of OpenStack.

We will cover the following topics in this chapter:

- Open vSwitch as L2 Switch with Network namespace
- Open vSwitch as an OpenFlow Switch interface with SDN Controller
- Open vSwitch and Mininet
- OpenStack Neutron architecture

OVS Networking with Linux Network namespace

The Linux operating system has a single routing table and global set of network interfaces. Network namespace scales this limitation by providing independent instances of network interfaces and routing tables. This feature enables network isolation and independent operation of multiple network instances. The following diagram depicts network topology with OVS interconnecting hosts isolated by network:

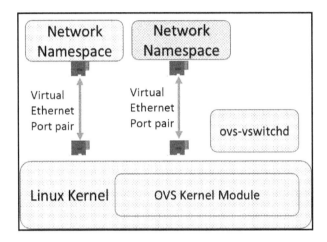

Figure 1: Network topology with OVS connecting with Network namespace hosts

The network interface within the namespace interconnects with **Virtual Ethernet Port** of open vSwitch via **Virtual Ethernet** (**VETH**) port pair. Virtual Ethernet ports are equivalent to a pair of physical Ethernet interfaces interconnected by a cable, albeit implemented purely using software. Virtual Ethernet is implemented as tunnel driver working at link layer (L2) connecting pair of Virtual Ethernet ports.

In this example, we will create two network namespaces and interconnect them with Open vSwitch. We will see how the Network namespace isolates the Network instance:

1. As the first step, let's create two Network namespaces one for each host, namely `blue_host` and `green_host`:

```
# ip netns add blue_host
# ip netns add green_host
# ip netns show
green_host
blue_host

# ip netns exec blue_host ip link show
1: lo: <LOOPBACK> mtu 65536 qdisc noop state DOWN mode DEFAULT group default qlen 1 link/
loopback 00:00:00:00:00:00 brd 00:00:00:00:00:00

# ip netns exec green_host ip link show
1: lo: <LOOPBACK> mtu 65536 qdisc noop state DOWN mode DEFAULT group default qlen 1 link/
loopback 00:00:00:00:00:00 brd 00:00:00:00:00:00
```

2. We will now add the links in the Network namespace to enable connectivity for the virtual hosts:

```
# ip link add blue_host-eth0 type veth peer name ovs_br-eth1
# ip link add green_host-eth0 type veth peer name ovs_br-eth2

# ip link show
11: ovs_br-eth1@blue_host-eth0: <BROADCAST,MULTICAST,M-DOWN> mtu 1500 qdisc noop state DOWN
mode DEFAULT group default qlen 1000
    link/ether 9a:2e:47:0b:b1:12 brd ff:ff:ff:ff:ff:ff
12: blue_host-eth0@ovs_br-eth1: <BROADCAST,MULTICAST,M-DOWN> mtu 1500 qdisc noop state DOWN
mode DEFAULT group default qlen 1000
    link/ether 46:1c:69:c8:b9:77 brd ff:ff:ff:ff:ff:ff
13: ovs_br-eth2@green_host-eth0: <BROADCAST,MULTICAST,M-DOWN> mtu 1500 qdisc noop state DOWN
mode DEFAULT group default qlen 1000
    link/ether ea:29:05:b8:cc:11 brd ff:ff:ff:ff:ff:ff
14: green_host-eth0@ovs_br-eth2: <BROADCAST,MULTICAST,M-DOWN> mtu 1500 qdisc noop state DOWN
mode DEFAULT group default qlen 1000
    link/ether 86:07:46:69:7a:27 brd ff:ff:ff:ff:ff:ff
```

3. Let us now add these links to the respective Network namespaces:

```
# ip link set blue_host-eth0 netns blue_host
# ip link set green_host-eth0 netns green_host

# ip netns exec blue_host ip link show
1: lo: <LOOPBACK> mtu 65536 qdisc noop state DOWN mode DEFAULT group default qlen 1
    link/loopback 00:00:00:00:00:00 brd 00:00:00:00:00:00
10: blue_host-eth0@if9: <BROADCAST,MULTICAST> mtu 1500 qdisc noop state DOWN mode DEFAULT
group default qlen 1000
    link/ether d2:c1:7a:c1:b0:64 brd ff:ff:ff:ff:ff:ff link-netnsid 0

# ip link set green_host-eth0 netns green_host
# ip netns exec green_host ip link show
1: lo: <LOOPBACK> mtu 65536 qdisc noop state DOWN mode DEFAULT group default qlen 1
    link/loopback 00:00:00:00:00:00 brd 00:00:00:00:00:00
14: green_host-eth0@if13: <BROADCAST,MULTICAST> mtu 1500 qdisc noop state DOWN mode DEFAULT
group default qlen 1000
    link/ether 86:07:46:69:7a:27 brd ff:ff:ff:ff:ff:ff link-netnsid 0
```

4. Verify the links move to the Network namespaces:

```
# ip link show
11: ovs_br-eth1@if12: <BROADCAST,MULTICAST> mtu 1500 qdisc noop state DOWN mode DEFAULT group
default qlen 1000
    link/ether 9a:2e:47:0b:b1:12 brd ff:ff:ff:ff:ff:ff link-netnsid 0
13: ovs_br-eth2@if14: <BROADCAST,MULTICAST> mtu 1500 qdisc noop state DOWN mode DEFAULT group
default qlen 1000
    link/ether ea:29:05:b8:cc:11 brd ff:ff:ff:ff:ff:ff link-netnsid 1
```

5. Configure IP address to the interfaces in the Network namespace as the next step:

```
# ip netns exec green_host ifconfig green_host-eth0 192.168.147.30
# ip netns exec blue_host ifconfig blue_host-eth0 192.168.147.20

# ip netns exec blue_host ifconfig
blue_host-eth0 Link encap:Ethernet  HWaddr 46:1c:69:c8:b9:77
          inet addr:192.168.147.20  Bcast:192.168.147.255  Mask:255.255.255.0
          UP BROADCAST MULTICAST  MTU:1500  Metric:1
          RX packets:0 errors:0 dropped:0 overruns:0 frame:0
          TX packets:0 errors:0 dropped:0 overruns:0 carrier:0
          collisions:0 txqueuelen:1000
          RX bytes:0 (0.0 B)  TX bytes:0 (0.0 B)

# ip netns exec green_host ifconfig
green_host-eth0 Link encap:Ethernet  HWaddr 86:07:46:69:7a:27
          inet addr:192.168.147.30  Bcast:192.168.147.255  Mask:255.255.255.0
          UP BROADCAST MULTICAST  MTU:1500  Metric:1
          RX packets:0 errors:0 dropped:0 overruns:0 frame:0
          TX packets:0 errors:0 dropped:0 overruns:0 carrier:0
          collisions:0 txqueuelen:1000
          RX bytes:0 (0.0 B)  TX bytes:0 (0.0 B)


# ifconfig
ovs_br-eth1 Link encap:Ethernet  HWaddr 9a:2e:47:0b:b1:12
          inet6 addr: fe80::982e:47ff:fe0b:b112/64 Scope:Link
          UP BROADCAST RUNNING MULTICAST  MTU:1500  Metric:1
          RX packets:8 errors:0 dropped:0 overruns:0 frame:0
          TX packets:23 errors:0 dropped:0 overruns:0 carrier:0
          collisions:0 txqueuelen:1000
          RX bytes:648 (648.0 B)  TX bytes:3606 (3.6 KB)

ovs_br-eth2 Link encap:Ethernet  HWaddr ea:29:05:b8:cc:11
          inet6 addr: fe80::e829:5ff:feb8:cc11/64 Scope:Link
          UP BROADCAST RUNNING MULTICAST  MTU:1500  Metric:1
          RX packets:6 errors:0 dropped:0 overruns:0 frame:0
          TX packets:20 errors:0 dropped:0 overruns:0 carrier:0
          collisions:0 txqueuelen:1000
          RX bytes:508 (508.0 B)  TX bytes:3156 (3.1 KB)
```

6. Ping the interface between the network namespace. We notice Ping does not succeed in confirming that the network interfaces between the Network namespace are isolated:

```
# ip netns exec blue_host ping -c5 192.168.147.30
PING 192.168.147.30 (192.168.147.30) 56(84) bytes of data.

--- 192.168.147.30 ping statistics ---
5 packets transmitted, 0 received, 100% packet loss, time 4031ms
```

7. Now let's interconnect the interfaces via Open vSwitch. By creating an OVS bridge and adding the VETH peer interfaces to the bridge:

```
# ovs-vsctl add-br ovs_br
# ovs-vsctl add-port ovs_br ovs_br-eth1
# ovs-vsctl add-port ovs_br ovs_br-eth2
# ovs-vsctl show
fed1601c-5c19-4679-9a48-3ce96ad1568f
    Bridge ovs_br
        Port "ovs_br-eth2"
            Interface "ovs_br-eth2"
        Port "ovs_br-eth1"
            Interface "ovs_br-eth1"
        Port ovs_br
            Interface ovs_br
                type: internal
```

8. Check the flow DB in the OVS to confirm that the network interfaces MAC is not learnt:

```
# ovs-appctl fdb/show ovs_br
 port  VLAN  MAC                   Age

# ovs-dpctl show
system@ovs-system:
        lookups: hit:0 missed:0 lost:0
        flows: 0
        masks: hit:0 total:0 hit/pkt:0.00
        port 0: ovs-system (internal)
        port 1: ofc-bridge (internal)
        port 2: ovs_br (internal)
        port 3: ovs_br-eth1
        port 4: ovs_br-eth2

# ovs-ofctl dump-flows ovs_br
NXST_FLOW reply (xid=0x4):
 cookie=0x0, duration=100.368s, table=0, n_packets=0, n_bytes=0, idle_age=100, priority=0
actions=NORMAL
```

9. Ping the interfaces in the network namespace, connected via OVS bridge:

```
# ip netns exec blue_host ping -c5 192.168.147.30
PING 192.168.147.30 (192.168.147.30) 56(84) bytes of data.
64 bytes from 192.168.147.30: icmp_seq=1 ttl=64 time=0.489 ms
---- 192.168.147.30 ping statistics ---
5 packets transmitted, 5 received, 0% packet loss, time 3998ms
rtt min/avg/max/mdev = 0.047/0.138/0.489/0.175 ms
```

10. We can now see that the **forwarding database** (**FDB**) in the OVS bridge `ovs_br` has learned the MAC addresses of the interfaces in the network namespace.

```
# ovs-appctl fdb/show ovs_br
 port  VLAN  MAC                 Age
    1     0  46:1c:69:c8:b9:77    21
    2     0  86:07:46:69:7a:27    21

# ovs-dpctl show
system@ovs-system:
        lookups: hit:9 missed:5 lost:0
        flows: 0
        masks: hit:19 total:0 hit/pkt:1.36
        port 0: ovs-system (internal)
        port 1: ofc-bridge (internal)
        port 2: ovs_br (internal)
        port 3: ovs_br-eth1
        port 4: ovs_br-eth2
```

11. Using the `ovs-ofctl` command, we will show that the packet count starts increasing.

```
# ovs-ofctl dump-flows ovs_br
NXST_FLOW reply (xid=0x4):
 cookie=0x0, duration=192.700s, table=0, n_packets=14, n_bytes=1148, idle_age=48, priority=0
actions=NORMAL
```

As we can see with the preceding example, Open vSwitch works like a regular MAC learning and forwarding switch when no controller is configured and OpenFlow rules are not programmed.

OVS networking with SDN controller

Now let us bring the OpenFlow controller to the configuration to manage the OVS. We will use a controller implemented on Ryu (pronounced *ree-yooh*), a component-based software-defined networking framework. Ryu provides software components with well-defined northbound Python APIs and it supports OpenFlow protocol towards southbound. Refer to `http://osrg.github.io/ryu/`.

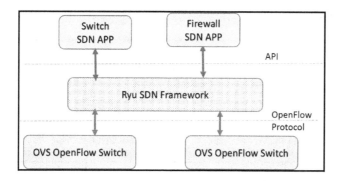

Figure 2: Ryu SDN framework

We will continue the example from the previous section, where we had two namespaces and two hosts. Let us first install the `ryu` SDN controller framework:

- Install directly using the `pip` command.

    ```
    $ sudo pip install ryu
    ```

- You can also install `ryu` from the source code.

    ```
    $ git clone git://github.com/osrg/ryu.git
    $ cd ryu; python ./setup.py install
    ```

In this example, we will add Open Flow controller and verify OVS Open Flow table updates. Ryu is running locally, hence we set the OVS controller to the local IP address.

1. The first step is to set the controller to the OVS bridge:

    ```
    # ovs-vsctl set-controller ovs_br tcp:127.0.0.1
    ```

2. The next step is to start the `ryu` OpenFlow controller:

```
/ryu# ./bin/ryu-manager --verbose ryu/app/simple_switch_13.py
loading app ryu/app/simple_switch_13.py

connected socket:<eventlet.greenio.base.GreenSocket object at 0xb6141cec> address:
('127.0.0.1', 44592)
hello ev <ryu.controller.ofp_event.EventOFPHello object at 0xb615206c>
move onto config mode
EVENT ofp_event->SimpleSwitch13 EventOFPSwitchFeatures
switch features ev
version=0x4,msg_type=0x6,msg_len=0x20,xid=0x356f99ff,OFPSwitchFeatures(auxiliary_id=0,capabili
ties=79,datapath_id=200625580741965L,n_buffers=256,n_tables=254)
move onto main mode
```

3. Ping the interfaces in the network namespace, connected via the OVS bridge and OpenFlow controller:

```
# ip netns exec blue_host ping -c1 192.168.147.30
PING 192.168.147.30 (192.168.147.30) 56(84) bytes of data.
64 bytes from 192.168.147.30: icmp_seq=1 ttl=64 time=4.28 ms
```

4. Check the OVS flow table controller using the `ovs-dpctl` command as shown in the following screenshot:

```
# ovs-dpctl show
system@ovs-system:
        lookups: hit:26 missed:14 lost:0
        flows: 0
        masks: hit:50 total:0 hit/pkt:1.25
        port 0: ovs-system (internal)
        port 1: ofc-bridge (internal)
        port 2: ovs_br (internal)
        port 3: ovs_br-eth1
        port 4: ovs_br-eth2
```

5. Verify that the OVS flow table is populated for the flow switching:

```
# ovs-ofctl dump-flows ovs_br
NXST_FLOW reply (xid=0x4):
 cookie=0x0, duration=68.497s, table=0, n_packets=6, n_bytes=532, idle_age=63,
priority=1,in_port=2,dl_dst=46:1c:69:c8:b9:77 actions=output:1
 cookie=0x0, duration=67.498s, table=0, n_packets=6, n_bytes=532, idle_age=63,
priority=1,in_port=1,dl_dst=86:07:46:69:7a:27 actions=output:2
 cookie=0x0, duration=216.595s, table=0, n_packets=2, n_bytes=196, idle_age=68, priority=0
actions=CONTROLLER:65535
```

6. We will now show you that the FDB is not populated:

```
# ovs-appctl fdb/show ovs_br
  port  VLAN  MAC                Age
```

7. Check `ryu` controller console for the flow program, and verify OpenFlow events:

```
EVENT ofp_event->SimpleSwitch13 EventOFPPacketIn
packet in 200625580741965 46:1c:69:c8:b9:77 86:07:46:69:7a:27 1
EVENT ofp_event->SimpleSwitch13 EventOFPPacketIn
packet in 200625580741965 86:07:46:69:7a:27 46:1c:69:c8:b9:77 2
EVENT ofp_event->SimpleSwitch13 EventOFPPacketIn
packet in 200625580741965 46:1c:69:c8:b9:77 86:07:46:69:7a:27 1
```

The `ping` traffic flows via OpenFlow-based on the flow rules programmed in the Open vSwitch by the SDN controller. FDB entries are not programmed.

8. Open vSwitch operates in *OpenFlow mode* when the controller programs the OpenFlow rules consisting of `match` and instructions with `action`.

We've seen the internal workings of network namespace-based virtual networking with OVS, how the OVS functions as regular MAC learning forwarding switch, and how it connects with an OpenFlow controller to receive inputs to program the OpenFlow flow tables. This understanding is the foundation of gaining insights into the internals of SDN virtual networking and OpenStack networking.

OVS and Mininet

Mininet is a tool that can emulate a realistic network on a single machine or VM with CLI support to interact with and API to customize, extend it. Mininet supports creating virtual hosts linking them to switch and hooking it up with a controller. It does all of this leveraging the same underlying components and techniques we used to in the previous example for network namespace-based virtual network. Refer to `http://mininet.org/ove rview/`.

You have two options to install the `mininet` tool:

- Using the Ubuntu `apt-get` command:

    ```
    $ sudo apt-get install mininet
    ```

- Install from the source code

    ```
    $ git clone git://github.com/mininet/mininet.git
    $ util/install.sh -fnv
    ```

We recommend using the first option.

In this example, we will create a Mininet setup and check the actions it performs to the Open vSwitch to emulate network.

Let us create a Mininet network with a switch and a couple of hosts, connect it to controller, and check out the underlying actions it does to accomplish the virtual network emulation.

1. The first step is to create a Mininet with a switch with three hosts, with Open vSwitch as the switch connected to external controller.

```
# mn --topo single,3 --mac --controller remote --switch ovsk
*** Creating network
*** Adding controller
*** Adding hosts:
h1 h2 h3
*** Adding switches:
s1
*** Adding links:
(h1, s1) (h2, s1) (h3, s1)
*** Configuring hosts
h1 h2 h3
*** Starting controller
c0
*** Starting 1 switches
s1 ...
*** Starting CLI:
mininet> h1 ping -c1 h2
PING 10.0.0.2 (10.0.0.2) 56(84) bytes of data.
64 bytes from 10.0.0.2: icmp_seq=1 ttl=64 time=3.33 ms

--- 10.0.0.2 ping statistics ---
1 packets transmitted, 1 received, 0% packet loss, time 0ms
rtt min/avg/max/mdev = 3.330/3.330/3.330/0.000 ms
mininet>
```

2. Let us check the configuration that Mininet creates using the OVS commands.

```
# ovs-vsctl show
fed1601c-5c19-4679-9a48-3ce96ad1568f
    Bridge "s1"
        Controller "ptcp:6634"
        Controller "tcp:127.0.0.1:6633"
            is_connected: true
        fail_mode: secure
        Port "s1"
            Interface "s1"
                type: internal
        Port "s1-eth2"
            Interface "s1-eth2"
        Port "s1-eth1"
            Interface "s1-eth1"
    ovs_version: "2.5.0"

# ovs-ofctl -O openflow13 dump-flows s1
OFPST_FLOW reply (OF1.3) (xid=0x2):
 cookie=0x0, duration=4.791s, table=0, n_packets=1, n_bytes=98, send_flow_rem reset_counts
in_port=2,dl_dst=00:00:00:00:00:01 actions=output:1
 cookie=0x0, duration=4.790s, table=0, n_packets=0, n_bytes=0, send_flow_rem reset_counts
in_port=1,dl_dst=00:00:00:00:00:02 actions=output:2
Check the Ryu controller for the Open Flow Control packets.
EVENT ofp_event->SimpleSwitch EventOFPPacketIn
packet in 1 00:00:00:00:00:01 ff:ff:ff:ff:ff:ff 1
EVENT ofp_event->SimpleSwitch EventOFPPacketIn
packet in 1 00:00:00:00:00:02 00:00:00:00:00:01 2
EVENT ofp_event->SimpleSwitch EventOFPPacketIn
packet in 1 00:00:00:00:00:01 00:00:00:00:00:02 1
```

3. Next, let us check the interfaces created by Mininet in the host OS.

```
# ifconfig
s1-eth1    Link encap:Ethernet  HWaddr 1e:d4:cb:30:62:10
           inet6 addr: fe80::1cd4:cbff:fe30:6210/64 Scope:Link
           UP BROADCAST RUNNING MULTICAST  MTU:1500  Metric:1
           RX packets:12 errors:0 dropped:0 overruns:0 frame:0
           TX packets:45 errors:0 dropped:0 overruns:0 carrier:0
           collisions:0 txqueuelen:1000
           RX bytes:920 (920.0 B)  TX bytes:5439 (5.4 KB)

s1-eth2    Link encap:Ethernet  HWaddr fa:0e:08:3f:7f:97
           inet6 addr: fe80::f80e:8ff:fe3f:7f97/64 Scope:Link
           UP BROADCAST RUNNING MULTICAST  MTU:1500  Metric:1
           RX packets:12 errors:0 dropped:0 overruns:0 frame:0
           TX packets:45 errors:0 dropped:0 overruns:0 carrier:0
           collisions:0 txqueuelen:1000
           RX bytes:920 (920.0 B)  TX bytes:5439 (5.4 KB)

s1-eth3    Link encap:Ethernet  HWaddr 8a:41:3a:1e:4d:23
           inet6 addr: fe80::8841:3aff:fe1e:4d23/64 Scope:Link
           UP BROADCAST RUNNING MULTICAST  MTU:1500  Metric:1
           RX packets:9 errors:0 dropped:0 overruns:0 frame:0
           TX packets:43 errors:0 dropped:0 overruns:0 carrier:0
           collisions:0 txqueuelen:1000
           RX bytes:738 (738.0 B)  TX bytes:5299 (5.2 KB)
```

We can see from the output of OVS that Mininet configures OVS switch connects to the external controller and creates interfaces based on easy-to-use Mininet commands.

Mininet supports a rich set of commands to emulate real network conditions, such as setting up link bandwidth, link delay, and loss characteristics.

Mininet provides APIs to specify nodes and link parameters, and define network objects and topology templates.

OVS connected to virtual machines

Let's now move our attention to networking with virtual machines with OVS as the switch interconnecting the VMs. The following diagram depicts two VMs interconnected via an Open vSwitch virtual switch:

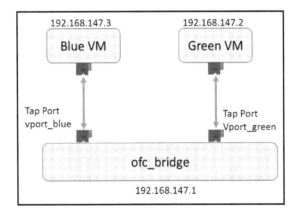

Figure 3: Open vSwitch network with VMs

We will start by creating an Open vSwitch bridge, add tap ports to it to hook VMs, and show how the VMs interconnect via OVS switch. The *tap* interfaces simulate a link layer operating with L2 packets such as Ethernet frames. These are virtual ports where virtual machines *plug in*.

1. We will create an OVS bridge and bring it up in order to assign IP address.

```
# ovs-vsctl add-br ofc_bridge

# ifconfig ofc_bridge up
# ip addr add 192.168.147.1/24 broadcast 192.168.147.255 dev ofc-bridge

# ifconfig ofc-bridge
ofc-bridge Link encap:Ethernet  HWaddr ca:df:97:f6:90:4d
           inet addr:192.168.147.1  Bcast:192.168.147.255  Mask:255.255.255.0
           inet6 addr: fe80::897:15ff:fe17:5002/64 Scope:Link
           UP BROADCAST RUNNING  MTU:1500  Metric:1
           RX packets:0 errors:0 dropped:0 overruns:0 frame:0
           TX packets:8 errors:0 dropped:0 overruns:0 carrier:0
           collisions:0 txqueuelen:0
           RX bytes:0 (0.0 B)  TX bytes:648 (648.0 B)
```

2. Next, we need to create and activate the `tap` interfaces:

```
# ip tuntap add mode tap vport_blue
# ip tuntap add mode tap vport_green

# ifconfig vport_green up
# ifconfig vport_blue up
```

3. The `add-port` option of `ovs-vsctl` command is used to add the virtual ports to the Open vSwitch.

```
# ovs-vsctl add-port ofc-bridge vport_blue
# ovs-vsctl add-port ofc-bridge vport_green
```

4. Let us now check the status of these ports.

```
# ifconfig
vport_blue Link encap:Ethernet  HWaddr 86:1a:6c:30:34:28
          UP BROADCAST RUNNING MULTICAST  MTU:1500  Metric:1
          RX packets:0 errors:0 dropped:0 overruns:0 frame:0
          TX packets:0 errors:0 dropped:0 overruns:0 carrier:0
          collisions:0 txqueuelen:1000
          RX bytes:0 (0.0 B)  TX bytes:0 (0.0 B)

vport_green Link encap:Ethernet  HWaddr da:b3:e4:a7:34:29
          UP BROADCAST RUNNING MULTICAST  MTU:1500  Metric:1
          RX packets:0 errors:0 dropped:0 overruns:0 frame:0
          TX packets:0 errors:0 dropped:0 overruns:0 carrier:0
          collisions:0 txqueuelen:1000
          RX bytes:0 (0.0 B)  TX bytes:0 (0.0 B)
```

5. We will now view the complete OVS bridge information.

```
# ovs-vsctl show
fed1601c-5c19-4679-9a48-3ce96ad1568f
    Bridge ofc-bridge
        Port vport_green
            Interface vport_green
        Port vport_blue
            Interface vport_blue
        Port ofc-bridge
            Interface ofc-bridge
                type: internal
    ovs_version: "2.5.0"
```

6. In order to create and configure virtual machines we will use CirrOS VM images. These images are very small and the VM instances boot quickly since minimal resources are needed. You can download the VM images from `http://download .cirros-cloud.net/`. You can create the VM instances using KVM-QEMU hypervisor as shown in the following screenshot:

```
kvm /opt/vm/green.img -vnc :2 -device virtio-net-pci,netdev=net0,mac='da:b3:e4:a7:34:29' -netdev
tap,id=net0,ifname=vport_green,script=no,downscript=no -name greenvm -daemonize

kvm /opt/vm/blue.img -vnc :3 -device virtio-net-pci,netdev=net0,mac='86:1a:6c:30:34:28' -netdev
tap,id=net0,ifname=vport_blue,script=no,downscript=no -name bluevm -daemonize
```

7. You can access the console for these VMs using the `vinagre` command on the Ubuntu host.

```
vinagre :2  [greenvm]
vinagre :3  [bluevm]
```

8. Set the IP address, gateway in console `greenvm` and set IP address, gateway in console `bluevm`:

```
ifconfig eth0 192.168.147.2 netmask 255.255.255.0 broadcast 192.168.147.255
route add default gw 192.168.147.1

ifconfig eth0 192.168.147.3 netmask 255.255.255.0 broadcast 192.168.147.255
route add default gw 192.168.147.1
```

9. Let us now test the connectivity of these VM instances via Open vSwitch. In console of the each VM, use the `ping` command to check connectivity to the gateway IP address `192.168.147.1`. Follow this up with a `ping` command to the IP address of the other VM.

10. Now check the **forwarding database** (**FDB**) entries for the MAC learning by the virtual switch.

```
# ovs-appctl fdb/show ofc-bridge

port  VLAN  MAC                Age
LOCAL    0  86:9c:87:c1:2f:4e   1
    2    0  86:1a:6c:30:34:28   1
    1    0  da:b3:e4:a7:34:29   1
# ovs-ofctl dump-flows ofc-bridge
NXST_FLOW reply (xid=0x4):
 cookie=0x0, duration=2610.157s, table=0, n_packets=7383, n_bytes=705236, idle_age=0, priority=0
actions=NORMAL

# ovs-dpctl show
system@ovs-system:
        lookups: hit:7201 missed:306 lost:0
        flows: 8
        masks: hit:13273 total:3 hit/pkt:1.77
        port 0: ovs-system (internal)
        port 1: ofc-bridge (internal)
        port 2: vport_green
        port 3: vport_blue
```

11. Check the interface statistics in the host OS:

```
# ifconfig
ofc-bridge Link encap:Ethernet  HWaddr 86:9c:87:c1:2f:4e
          inet addr:192.168.147.1  Bcast:192.168.147.255  Mask:255.255.255.0
          inet6 addr: fe80::849c:87ff:fec1:2f4e/64 Scope:Link
          UP BROADCAST RUNNING MULTICAST  MTU:1500  Metric:1
          RX packets:3585 errors:0 dropped:18 overruns:0 frame:0
          TX packets:3650 errors:0 dropped:0 overruns:0 carrier:0
          collisions:0 txqueuelen:1
          RX bytes:290724 (290.7 KB)  TX bytes:348990 (348.9 KB)

vport_blue Link encap:Ethernet  HWaddr 86:1a:6c:30:34:28
          UP BROADCAST RUNNING MULTICAST  MTU:1500  Metric:1
          RX packets:1810 errors:0 dropped:0 overruns:0 frame:0
          TX packets:1936 errors:0 dropped:0 overruns:0 carrier:0
          collisions:0 txqueuelen:1000
          RX bytes:172698 (172.6 KB)  TX bytes:186518 (186.5 KB)

vport_green Link encap:Ethernet  HWaddr da:b3:e4:a7:34:29
          UP BROADCAST RUNNING MULTICAST  MTU:1500  Metric:1
          RX packets:1793 errors:0 dropped:0 overruns:0 frame:0
          TX packets:1859 errors:0 dropped:0 overruns:0 carrier:0
          collisions:0 txqueuelen:1000
          RX bytes:171144 (171.1 KB)  TX bytes:179262 (179.2 KB)
```

In the preceding example, OVS interconnects the traffic between the virtual machines. The OpenStack networking component (Neutron) uses a similar mechanism underneath to automate the creation of virtual networks between the virtual hosts. Open vSwitch (OVS) is the most popular virtual switch in OpenStack deployment.

OpenStack Neutron

Neutron has highly modular, open, and extensible architecture consisting of plugins, agents, and services. Neutron plugins are classified into core and service plugins. Core plugins primarily deal with L2 connectivity and IP address management, while service plugins support services such as routing (L3), firewalls, and load-balancing services.

Plugins in Neutron allow the extension and customization of the Neutron's functionality. For instance, network equipment vendors can implement custom plugins to enable inter-operability between OpenStack Neutron and their specific software and hardware. The Neutron agents implement very specific networking functionalities. Examples include DHCP agent and L3 agent. The main Neutron server (and the plugins) communicate with Neutron agents. Refer to `http://docs.openstack.org/admin-guide/networking-introd uction.html`.

The definition of APIs for network objects and services coupled with plugin design enables interoperability between routers, switches, virtual switches, and software-defined networking (SDN) controllers from both open source and commercial network equipment vendors. Neutron provides *networking as a service* for other OpenStack components.

The following diagram depicts the OpenStack Neutron architecture:

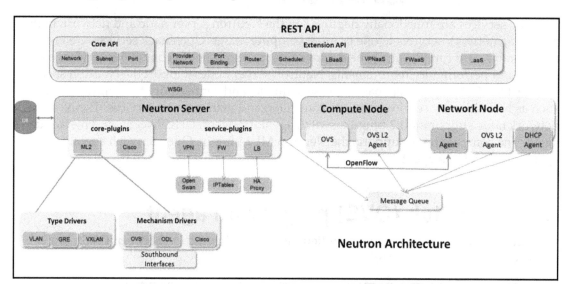

Figure 4: High-level Neutron Architecture

Neutron includes the following core components:

- **API server**: The neutron-server daemon provides common application interface for various networking abstractions supported by Neutron. It provides APIs to create and manage network objects, such as networks, subnets, ports and network services such as Layer 2 networking, L3 routing between Layer 2 networks and gateways to external networks, NAT, load balancing, firewalls, and virtual private networks.

- **Networking plug-in**: ML2 is the OpenStack Networking core plug-in. It supports type driver to maintain type specific network state and mechanism drivers for applying configuration to specific networking mechanisms. Type driver performs provider network validation and tenant network allocation.

- **Neutron agents**: Agents implement the actual networking functionality closely associated to specific technologies and the corresponding plugins. Agents receive messages and instructions from the Neutron server (via plugins or directly) on the message bus.

- **Messaging queue**: To route RPC requests between the Neutron server and Neutron agents and between the Neutron agents.

Neutron services layout

Neutron services are functionally deployed in the Neutron server node and network node providing network services to one or more compute nodes. OpenStack services are highly configurable, and can physically be deployed in the server nodes combining services as per scaling and performance requirements. Neutron server nodes support the Neutron server service, the ML2 plug-in, databases, message queue, and connectivity to common services such as NTP, identity service, compute controller, and management services. The Neutron network node supports ML2 plug-in, switch agent, L3 agent, DHCP agent, and metadata agent. The compute node supports the Neutron ML2 plug-in, Open vSwitch agent, L3 agent, and metadata agent.

Open vSwitch (OVS) plugin and agent

The following diagram depicts a simplified view of the interaction between OVS plugins and agents:

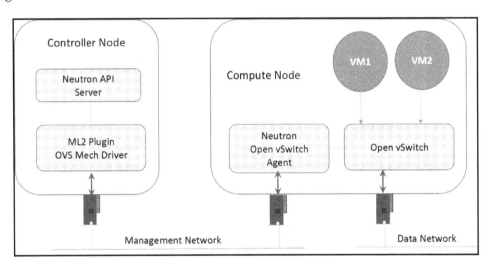

Figure 5: Neutron Open vSwitch Agent interface

Neutron API Server receives commands via REST API clients such as Horizon, the OpenStack GUI. The API server invokes the **ML2 Plugin** to processes the request. The passes the request the configured OVS mechanism driver. The OVS driver constructs an RPC message and directs it towards the OVS agent on the intended **Compute Node** over the **Management Network** interface. The OVS agent in the **Compute Node** communicates with the local OVS instance to program it as per the instructions in the received command.

Summary

In this chapter, we delved into the building blocks of OpenFlow-based networking. We have learned about lightweight networking technologies such as network namespaces, and how they inter-connect via Open vSwitch as reference OpenFlow switch. We have seen how underlying virtual switch infrastructure is common for full-fledged VM networks. We have also seen how Open vSwitch interfaces with SDN controllers. We covered the overall architecture of OpenStack Neutron. Finally, we covered the high-level interaction between OpenStack and OVS.

This knowledge will help us understand the functioning of SDN controllers, which are covered in the subsequent chapters as we dive into the internals of Neutron, OpenStack network-as-a-service component.

5
Getting Started with OpenDaylight

In Chapter 2, *Introduction to Software-Defined Networking*, we showed how SDN solves the challenges faced by traditional networking when it is used in a cloud network infrastructure. We understood the need for a distributed control plane and centralized management in modern data center networking designs. It was highlighted that SDN technologies must provide abstractions, programmatic APIs, and multi-vendor support.

Let's now focus our attention on a specific SDN platform called **OpenDaylight** (**ODL**). OpenDaylight is an open source SDN platform developed by a community supported by key companies from the technology industry. The ODL project was launched in the year 2013 and its most recent release is named **Beryllium**. In a short span of time ODL has become the SDN and NFV platform of choice for the industry.

ODL addresses the key needs for SDN by supporting network abstractions, rich APIs, and multi-vendor support. Its architecture helps support large-scale and a diverse set of devices and network protocols. ODL acts as a controller for distributed control planes and also provides a user interface and APIs for centralized management. It acts as on orchestrator for **Virtual Network Functions** (**VNF**).

In this chapter, we will start with an introduction to ODL, its architecture, and then explore ODL integration with OVS. We will conclude the chapter with a quick introduction to using ODL in an OpenStack environment. We will cover the following topics in this chapter:

- Introduction to ODL
- Architecture of ODL
- Installing ODL
- Using ODL to manage is Open vSwitch (OVS)
- ODL and OpenStack

Introduction to OpenDaylight

ODL project started in 2013 as an industry effort to decouple networking hardware and software. The intention is to create a common industry-supported SDN platform and allow end users to build powerful networking applications with a plug-n-play architecture.

ODL is an open source project under the Linux foundation supported by networking vendors and operators who want to leverage SDN capabilities and handle specific networking use cases. It has a flexible architecture that allows new networking hardware to be easily integrated into the SDN framework.

The most recent release of ODL is named Beryllium and was released in early 2016. You can visit `http://www.opendaylight.org` for the latest updates about ODL.

Architecture of OpenDaylight

ODL supports a layered architecture with clear integration points and APIs that allow end users and networking vendors to participate in the power SDN capabilities of ODL. The *southbound* interface to ODL ensures that networking technologies and hardware from diverse vendors can be leveraged using ODL. The *northbound* interface provides APIs for end users and other cloud technologies such as OpenStack. The following block diagram captures the architecture of ODL:

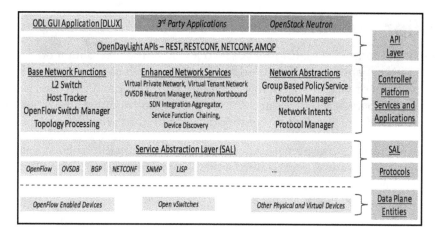

Figure 1: ODL architecture overview

In a cloud deployment, other components such as compute and storage also play a critical role, in addition to networking. While ODL acts as the SDN platform while building the cloud infrastructure, it is critical for ODL to integrate with platforms such as OpenStack to provide seamless user experience while operating the cloud. Specifically, ODL needs to be integrated with OpenStack Neutron to provide an SDN-based network for the cloud.

Let's now look at some important aspects of the ODL architecture.

REST API

As part of the northbound interface, ODL supports very important APIs. These RESTful APIs are primarily meant for integrating with platforms such as OpenStack (Neutron) and also custom applications. The REST APIs are also used to build a graphical user interface or GUI for ODL. Programmability is one of the primary requirements for SDN platforms and the REST API of ODL allows very specific networking applications to be built outside ODL in order to leverage the information and capabilities available in ODL.

Controller platform

The purpose of the controller platform layer is to leverage the SAL data model and provide fundamental SDN capabilities and networking functions such as topology, performance monitoring, physical or virtual switch management, and ARP handling. This is the layer that acts as the glue between southbound interfaces and northbound interfaces. The REST APIs exposed by ODL are handled by components within the controller platform.

The controller platform also supports use case-specific functionality such as *virtual tenant network* manager. This is a useful capability while integrating with cloud platforms such as OpenStack. Similarly, for telecom service providers who use real networking devices heavily, functions such as the BGP based path computation engine is supported in ODL.

SAL

The **Service Abstraction Layer** (**SAL**) is the most critical layer of ODL. As seen earlier SDN platforms need to provide a centralized control plane while the data plane stays distributed. Being an open source project, ODL is required to support data planes from a multitude of hardware vendors. In addition to physical networking devices, ODL will also have to manage the data planes of virtual networking devices.

The main purpose of SAL is to map a diverse set of networking technologies into a common abstracted data model. All the controller services of ODL operate on this abstract data model, thus creating a vendor-neutral SDN controller. This approach also allows vendors and networking technologies to easily integrate themselves with ODL. SAL and the different protocols used to communicate with networking devices together make up the southbound interface for ODL.

Protocol plugins

ODL has built-in support for different protocols, using which it can communicate with networking devices. Using pluggable architecture support for new protocols can be easily added by writing new plugins. The most popular plugins are OVSDB, OpenFlow, and Netconf. These protocols are used for managing physical and virtual Layer 2 switching devices. BGP is a well-established protocol for communicating with routers. The following diagram shows how ODL uses OpenFlow *protocol plugin* to enable forwarding rules:

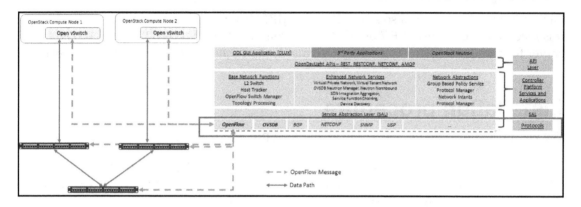

OpenFlow plugin interaction with physical and virtual switches for packet forwarding

The OpenFlow protocol plugin communicates with **Open vSwitch** (virtual switch) on the compute nodes and with the physical devices connected to the compute nodes. This allows appropriate forwarding rules to be configured to enable data flow.

The physical switches shown in the preceding diagram represent devices that support OpenFlow protocol messages.

Installing ODL

Having understood the basic architecture of ODL, let's now turn our attention towards installation of ODL. In this section, we will also show you how to install a few components inside ODL and then how to log in to the ODL GUI.

Version

The most recent version of ODL at the time of writing is Beryllium 0.4.2 SR2. The pre-built packages can be downloaded from `https://www.OpenDaylight.org/downloads`. We recommend that you download the pre-built TAR file.

Prerequisites

ODL is built using Java and so a Java Runtime (JRE) is required to use ODL. For Beryllium, it is recommended to use JRE 7 or JRE 8. We recommend using a 64-bit Ubuntu-based server for trying out ODL. You can use VirtualBox to create this server as a virtual machine.

Installation procedure

We will now show you how to install ODL using prebuilt packages:

1. Download and copy the pre-built package to an appropriate location.
2. Execute the `gunzip` command to uncompress the pre-built package. This will create the TAR ball package in the same directory:

```
openstack@openstack-base:~$ ls -al distribution-karaf-0.4.2-Beryllium-SR2.*
-rw-r--r-- 1 openstack openstack 295351385 May 29 16:22 distribution-karaf-0.4.2-Beryllium-SR2.tar.gz
openstack@openstack-base:~$
openstack@openstack-base:~$ gunzip distribution-karaf-0.4.2-Beryllium-SR2.tar.gz
openstack@openstack-base:~$
openstack@openstack-base:~$
openstack@openstack-base:~$ ls -al distribution-karaf-0.4.2-Beryllium-SR2.*
-rw-r--r-- 1 openstack openstack 344627200 May 29 16:22 distribution-karaf-0.4.2-Beryllium-SR2.tar
openstack@openstack-base:~$
openstack@openstack-base:~$
```

3. Extract the contents of the TAR package using the `tar` command, as shown in the following screenshot:

```
openstack@openstack-base:~$ tar xvf distribution-karaf-0.4.2-Beryllium-SR2.tar
```

4. The contents of the ODL Beryllium release are now available once the `tar` command completes:

```
openstack@openstack-base:~$ ls -al distribution-karaf-0.4.2-Beryllium-SR2*
-rw-r--r--  1 openstack openstack 344627200 May 29 16:22 distribution-karaf-0.4.2-Beryllium-SR2.tar

distribution-karaf-0.4.2-Beryllium-SR2:
total 56
drwxrwxr-x 10 openstack openstack  4096 May 29 16:26 .
drwxr-xr-x  6 openstack openstack  4096 May 29 16:26 ..
drwxr-xr-x  2 openstack openstack  4096 May  6 21:05 bin
drwxr-xr-x  2 openstack openstack  4096 May 29 16:26 configuration
drwxr-xr-x  3 openstack openstack  4096 May  7 07:33 data
drwxr-xr-x  2 openstack openstack  4096 May 29 16:26 deploy
drwxr-xr-x  2 openstack openstack  4096 May 29 16:26 etc
drwxr-xr-x  2 openstack openstack  4096 May 29 16:26 externalapps
drwxr-xr-x  5 openstack openstack  4096 May 29 16:26 lib
-rw-r--r--  1 openstack openstack 11266 May  6 20:27 LICENSE
drwxr-xr-x 27 openstack openstack  4096 May 29 16:26 system
-rw-r--r--  1 openstack openstack   329 May  6 21:05 version.properties
openstack@openstack-base:~$
```

5. Open Daylight uses Apache Decanter to package, install, and manage components. In order to start ODL, start Decanter `karaf` command, as shown in the following screenshot:

```
openstack@openstack-base:~/distribution-karaf-0.4.2-Beryllium-SR2$ ./bin/karaf
OpenJDK 64-Bit Server VM warning: ignoring option MaxPermSize=512m; support was removed in 8.0
```

```
Hit '<tab>' for a list of available commands
and '[cmd] --help' for help on a specific command.
Hit '<ctrl-d>' or type 'system:shutdown' or 'logout' to shutdown OpenDaylight.

opendaylight-user@root>
```

6. The pre-built package of ODL comes installed with basic yet key components. You can use the `feature:list -i` command, as shown in the following screenshot:

```
opendaylight-user@root>feature:list -i
Name            | Version | Installed | Repository      | Description
standard        | 3.0.3   | x         | standard-3.0.3  | Karaf standard feature
config          | 3.0.3   | x         | standard-3.0.3  | Provide OSGi ConfigAdmin support
region          | 3.0.3   | x         | standard-3.0.3  | Provide Region Support
package         | 3.0.3   | x         | standard-3.0.3  | Package commands and mbeans
http            | 3.0.3   | x         | standard-3.0.3  | Implementation of the OSGI HTTP Service
war             | 3.0.3   | x         | standard-3.0.3  | Turn Karaf as a full WebContainer
kar             | 3.0.3   | x         | standard-3.0.3  | Provide KAR (KARaf archive) support
ssh             | 3.0.3   | x         | standard-3.0.3  | Provide a SSHd server on Karaf
management      | 3.0.3   | x         | standard-3.0.3  | Provide a JMX MBeanServer and a set of MBeans in K
```

7. This completes the basic installation of ODL. In order to use ODL for practical purposes, we need to install additional packages such as DLUX GUI and L2 Switch.

Installing DLUX GUI

To install DLUX GUI, perform the following steps:

1. Use the `feature:install <features>` command to install DLUX GUI, as shown in the following screenshot:

```
opendaylight-user@root>feature:install odl-dlux-all
opendaylight-user@root>
```

2. Once DLUX is installed, you can open a web browser and navigate to `http://<controller-ip-address>:8181/index.html`. This will open the login form of ODL, as shown in the following screenshot:

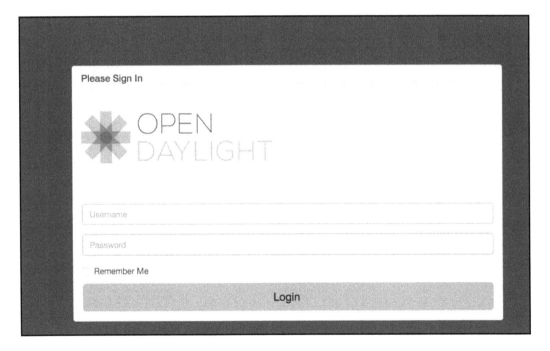

3. Use `admin/admin` as the **Username** and **Password** to log in to ODL.

4. Click on the **Nodes** link on the left navigation bar. This will show an empty table on the right-hand side. Once ODL starts managing networking devices, they will show inside the table.

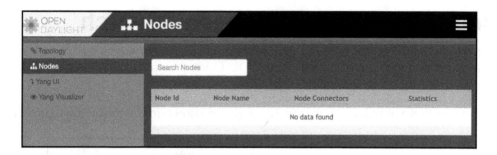

As seen in the preceding screenshot, we can now use ODL and its capabilities using the DLUX web UI package. However, in order to manage networking devices, we need additional components to be installed in ODL.

Installing the L2 Switch package

The L2 Switch feature of ODL provides layer 2 switch functionality. The main purpose of L2 Switch is to handle ARP, detect and remove loops, and track MAC addresses and IP addresses. This package is needed to model a physical or virtual layer 2 switch inside ODL so that the switch can be managed using ODL.

Use the `feature:install <features>` command to install L2 switch packages, as shown in the following screenshot. Once the installation is complete you can use `feature:list -i` command to confirm that L2 switch packages are installed.

```
opendaylight-user@root>feature:install odl-l2switch-all
opendaylight-user@root>feature:list -i
Name                          | Version             | Installed | Repository                          | Description
standard                      | 3.0.3               | x         | standard-3.0.3                      | Karaf standard feature
config                        | 3.0.3               | x         | standard-3.0.3                      | Provide OSGi ConfigAdmin support
region                        | 3.0.3               | x         | standard-3.0.3                      | Provide Region Support
package                       | 3.0.3               | x         | standard-3.0.3                      | Package commands and mbeans
http                          | 3.0.3               | x         | standard-3.0.3                      | Implementation of the OSGI HTTP Service
war                           | 3.0.3               | x         | standard-3.0.3                      | Turn Karaf as a full WebContainer
kar                           | 3.0.3               | x         | standard-3.0.3                      | Provide KAR (KARaf archive) support
ssh                           | 3.0.3               | x         | standard-3.0.3                      | Provide a SSHd server on Karaf
management                    | 3.0.3               | x         | standard-3.0.3                      | Provide a JMX MBeanServer and a set of MBeans in K
odl-openflowjava-protocol     | 0.7.2-Beryllium-SR2 | x         | odl-openflowjava-0.7.2-Beryllium-SR2| OpenDaylight :: Openflow Java :: Protocol
odl-l2switch-all              | 0.3.2-Beryllium-SR2 | x         | l2switch-0.3.2-Beryllium-SR2        | OpenDaylight :: L2Switch :: All
odl-l2switch-switch           | 0.3.2-Beryllium-SR2 | x         | l2switch-0.3.2-Beryllium-SR2        | OpenDaylight :: L2Switch :: Switch
odl-l2switch-hosttracker      | 0.3.2-Beryllium-SR2 | x         | l2switch-0.3.2-Beryllium-SR2        | OpenDaylight :: L2Switch :: HostTracker
odl-l2switch-addresstracker   | 0.3.2-Beryllium-SR2 | x         | l2switch-0.3.2-Beryllium-SR2        | OpenDaylight :: L2Switch :: AddressTracker
odl-l2switch-arphandler       | 0.3.2-Beryllium-SR2 | x         | l2switch-0.3.2-Beryllium-SR2        | OpenDaylight :: L2Switch :: ArpHandler
odl-l2switch-loopremover      | 0.3.2-Beryllium-SR2 | x         | l2switch-0.3.2-Beryllium-SR2        | OpenDaylight :: L2Switch :: LoopRemover
odl-l2switch-packethandler    | 0.3.2-Beryllium-SR2 | x         | l2switch-0.3.2-Beryllium-SR2        | OpenDaylight :: L2Switch :: PacketHandler
```

This completes, installation and configuration of a minimal ODL setup. As seen in the architecture diagram ODL, supports many other capabilities, and as an end user, you can install and use the features that you require.

Using ODL to manage Open vSwitch

Having installed and configured ODL with the preceding features, let's put the setup to use by managing Open vSwitch instances using ODL. Open vSwitch or OVS as it is popularly called is a virtual switch that supports OpenFlow protocols.

To accomplish this, we will implement a topology, as shown in the following diagram:

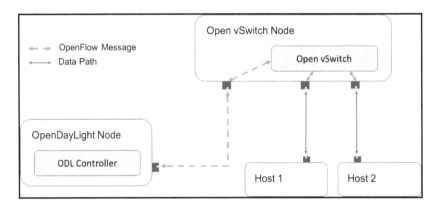

Network topology to show ODL managing Open vSwitch

In the preceding topology, we have an **ODL Controller** node. This is the node where ODL is installed and configured with DLUX and L2 Switch packages. The second most important node is the **Open vSwitch** node. This is a simple Linux host running **Open vSwitch**. We will attach two interfaces on this node to the **Open vSwitch** instance, and two hosts will be connected to the two interfaces on the **Open vSwitch** node.

Installing and configuring OVS

We have already shown how to set up and configure an ODL node. Let's now proceed to set up an Open vSwitch node. The following steps assume that the Open vSwitch node is running Ubuntu server edition 15.10 or higher.

1. Install Open vSwitch packages on the Open vSwitch node as follows:

```
openstack@openstack-base:~$ sudo apt-get install openvswitch-switch
```

2. Add an OVS bridge called `br-test` and add two interfaces as per the topology diagram. Depending on your server, you will have to choose the appropriate network interfaces:

```
openstack@openstack-base:~$
openstack@openstack-base:~$ sudo ovs-vsctl add-br br-test
openstack@openstack-base:~$ _

openstack@openstack-base:~$ sudo ovs-vsctl add-port br-test enp0s8
openstack@openstack-base:~$
openstack@openstack-base:~$ sudo ovs-vsctl add-port br-test enp0s9
```

3. Since these interfaces are bound to an OVS bridge, these should not have any IP addresses assigned to it. Edit the `/etc/network/interfaces` file and ensure that the following entries are added:

```
auto enp0s8
iface enp0s8 inet manual

auto enp0s9
iface enp0s9 inet manual
```

4. Finally, bring up the two interfaces as follows:

```
openstack@openstack-base:~$ sudo ifup enp0s8
openstack@openstack-base:~$
openstack@openstack-base:~$ sudo ifup enp0s9
```

5. At this stage, the OVS is configured to forward traffic between `enp0s8` and `enp0s9`. If end hosts Host 1 and Host 2 are now connected to these interface, data path traffic will flow via the Open vSwitch (`br-test`).

Managing OVS Using OpenDaylight

Next, we will show you how to manage the OVS instance called `br-test` using an ODL controller. This will complete the whole setup and configuration:

1. On the Open vSwitch node, set the ODL controller IP address on the OVS bridge instance. as shown in the following screenshot. In your setup, the IP address of the ODL controller may be different. By default, ODL listens to port `6633` for OpenFlow protocol messages.

```
openstack@openstack-base:~$ sudo ovs-vsctl set-controller br-test tcp:192.168.56.101:6633
```

2. Once the preceding command is successfully executed, the OVS instance `br-test` will send OpenFlow messages to the ODL controller. We can now log in to our ODL DLUX GUI and view details about the OVS and the hosts.

3. Open a browser and navigate to `http://<controller-ip-address>:8181/index.html#/topology`. This will display OVS and the host topology, as shown in the following screenshot:

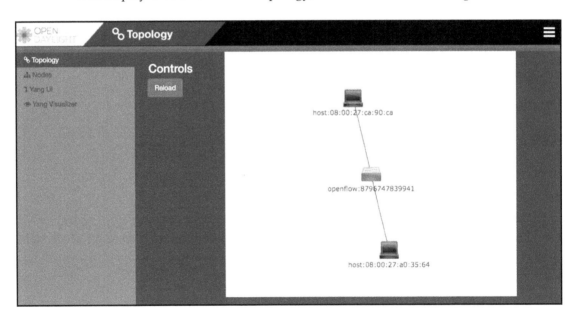

4. In the left navigation bar, click on the **Nodes**. This will show a tabular view of the OVS instance. The number **3** indicates the number of ports on OVS instance:

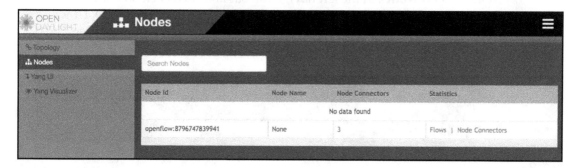

5. Click on the Node connectors number (in this case **3**) to view additional details such as the MAC address of each connector or port as shown in the following screenshot:

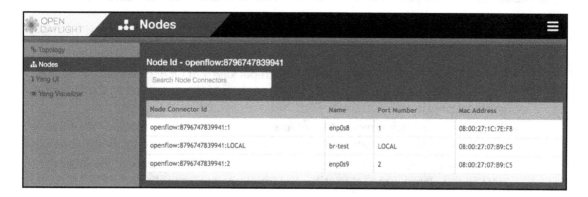

6. If there is data traffic going between Host 1 and 2, the traffic statistics are collected by the OVS instance. We can view these statistics using ODL GUI as well. Click on **Nodes** in the left navigation bar and then click on **Node Connectors** under the **Statistics** column for OVS instance. The DLUX UI will show details such as packets transmitted and received, bytes transmitted and received on each port/connector of the OVS instance.

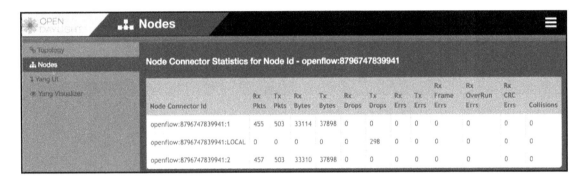

The preceding steps showed how quickly we could manage an Open vSwitch virtual switch using ODL. There are several important points to highlight at this stage:

- We explicitly installed only the L2 Switch packages in ODL. Internally based on dependencies ODL automatically installed the SAL layer as well as the OpenFlow protocol plugin.
- Since Open vSwitch support OpenFlow, our ODL controller instance was able to the OVS bridge and created an abstracted model inside the controller platform.
- The topology modules of the controller platform then were able to leverage the data in the abstract model to stitch the topology connectivity of the OVS virtual switch.

ODL and OpenStack

By now, you should have a fair idea about how ODL can manage virtual switches especially Open vSwitch. Now let's take a brief look at how ODL and OpenStack work together to provide powerful SDN capabilities for cloud operators.

OVS is the most popular virtual switch used in OpenStack-based clouds. OVS is used inside OpenStack compute nodes to provide virtual network connectivity to VM instances. However, cloud infrastructure is highly elastic in nature, it can be scaled up or down on demand. This means that the step of associating an OVS to ODL cannot be done manually. It needs to be automated.

In addition, in OpenStack-based clouds, different tenants share the same OVS virtual switch but their data traffic needs to be isolated. One of the main drivers for isolation is that different tenants may be using overlapping IP addresses in their network. This multi-tenancy requirement makes it harder to configure each OVS instance manually. Therefore, all the operations on OVS must be performed as part of OpenStack commands.

With the help of a simple diagram, we will show how OVS is leveraged using ODL in an OpenStack-based cloud. The following diagram shows a highly simplified OpenStack setup along with ODL controller.

In a normal situation, when OpenStack tenants/users make requests for creating a network or a subnet, the corresponding request is handled by the Neutron server running inside the OpenStack controller node:

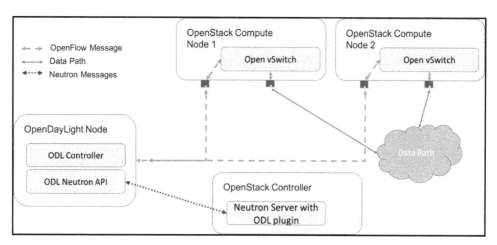

Flow of messages between OpenStack nodes and ODL

In the preceding deployment, the Neutron server is configured with an ODL plugin. When Neutron server receives a request allocate network resources, it forwards the request to ODL's Neutron API using the ODL Neutron plugin. The **ODL Neutron API**, in turn will use the **ODL Controller** platform and OpenFlow plugins to program the OVS instances running on the OpenStack compute nodes.

From the end user perspective, the initial operation was performed using OpenStack GUI but thanks to the rich APIs both in OpenStack as well as ODL, the actual handling of the user request is *transparently and automatically* handled by ODL. Therefore, ODL is able to act as the centralized network controller for OVS in an OpenStack environment. And since ODL has a flexible, pluggable architecture, it can also control other virtual and physical networking entities in this scenario.

Summary

This chapter provided an introduction to ODL controller. After covering the ODL architecture in brief we showed how to install and configure an ODL controller. With the help of a simple example, we showed how ODL can manage Open vSwitch. With OVS being the most used virtual switch in OpenStack deployment, this step was important in understanding the relationship between ODL and OpenStack. In the next chapter, we will delve deeper into the ODL and OpenStack integration. In addition to Neutron integration, we will also cover ODL specific topics such as Virtual Tenant Manager.

6
Using OpenDaylight with OpenStack

In Chapter 5, *Getting Started with OpenDaylight*, we introduced OpenDaylight as an open source SDN project that supports SDN protocols such as OpenFlow and OVSDB. In a cloud environment, ODL interacts with OpenStack Neutron to provide the network abstractions necessary for flexible and scalable application deployment. In the previous chapter, we also discussed the OpenDaylight and OpenStack integration in brief.

In this chapter, we will delve deeper into the integration of the ODL and OpenStack environment. Being an SDN solution, OpenDaylight integrates with OpenStack Neutron and handles the network provisioning requests. While Neutron is designed to support various virtual networking technologies, the integration with ODL is implemented using Open vSwitch-based virtual networking. This is because ODL uses OpenFlow and OVSDB protocols to configure virtual networks on the OpenStack compute nodes.

We will cover the following topics in this chapter:

- Integrating OpenDaylight with OpenStack
- Configuring OpenStack Neutron for ODL
- Introducing to Virtual Tenant Network in ODL
- Virtual Tenant Network and OpenStack

Integrating OpenDaylight with OpenStack

As more and more applications are hosted on cloud-based infrastructure, there is a growing need for building networks that are independent of the underlying network hardware. This promise is realized using SDN technologies such as OpenDaylight. However, as a standalone SDN platform, ODL can provide only a subset of the capabilities needed for a cloud infrastructure.

OpenStack can be considered as a collection of services that leverage underlying networks, hypervisor hosts, and storage devices to create an open cloud platform. As introduced in Chapter 1, *OpenStack Networking in a Nutshell*, Neutron is the OpenStack service that handles network provisioning requests from cloud users. Therefore, in order to leverage ODL in a cloud infrastructure, it must integrate with OpenStack Neutron.

Components of ODL and Neutron integration

Neutron can provide networking services to OpenStack users using a combination of virtual and physical networking platforms. For example, **Open vSwitch** (**OVS**) is the most popular virtual switch in an OpenStack deployment. Other examples of virtual switches are Linux bridge, vRouter from OpenContrail, and so on. The plugin and driver-based architecture of Neutron ensures that OVS works with physical network hardware from different vendors.

The following diagram shows OpenStack Networking components without OpenDaylight:

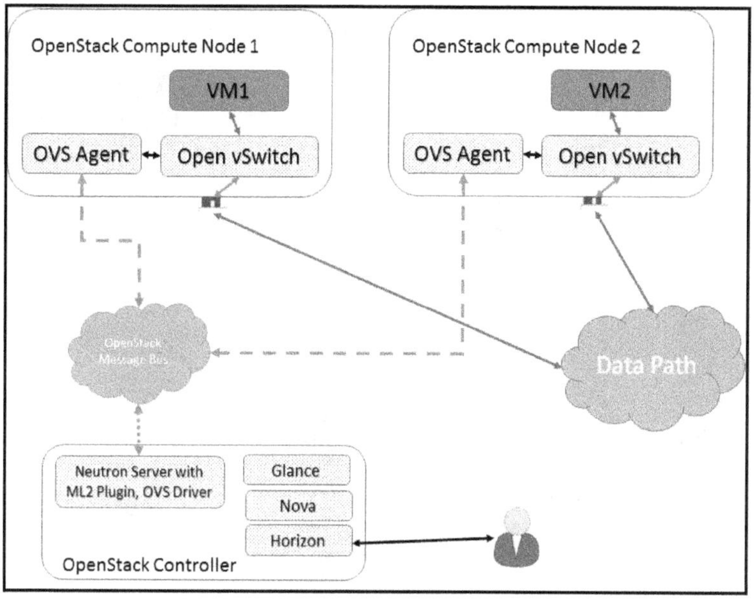

Figure 1: OpenStack Networking without ODL

As shown in *Figure 1*, when the user creates OpenStack Networking entities such as a network or subnet using the GUI, the request is first processed by the Horizon service on the controller node. The request is then delegated to the Neutron service. In this setup, Neutron is configured to use the **ML2 Plugin** with **OVS Driver**. The network provisioning request is handled by the **OVS Driver**, which sends messages to **OVS Agent** running on the compute nodes. The **OVS agent** then configures the virtual network on the compute node using **Open vSwitch**. The virtual machines are then bound to these OVS bridges in order for data traffic to flow through.

The following diagram shows how OpenStack Networking looks when ODL is integrated:

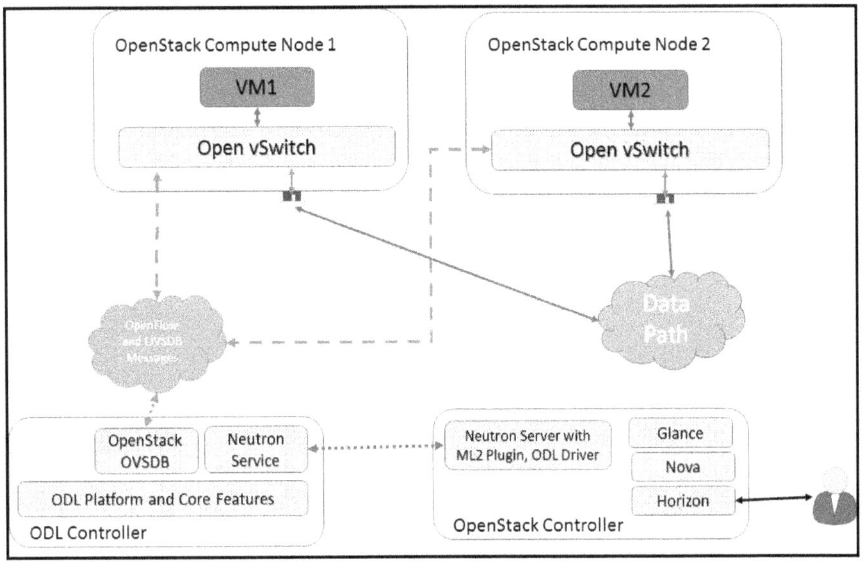

Figure 2: OpenStack Networking with OpenDaylight

As seen in *Figure 2*, Neutron is now the configured **ODL Driver** instead of OVS Driver. The OpenDaylight ML2 driver uses REST APIs to send messages to the ODL controller. The ODL controller then uses OVSDB and OpenFlow protocols to directly configure the OVS bridges and ports on the compute node.

In this scenario, the OVS agents on the compute nodes are no longer needed. Also, each OVS system on the compute nodes is directly managed and controlled by the ODL controller, so Neutron only needs to communicate with OpenDaylight's Neutron REST API.

Configuring OpenStack Neutron for ODL

In this section, we will look at the specific steps to enable OpenStack and ODL integration. We will show how users can make a transition from an OpenStack-only setup (*Figure 1*) to an OpenStack + ODL setup (*Figure 2*).

The following steps have been tested on the latest release of OpenDaylight, the Beryllium SR2, and the Mitaka release of OpenStack on the Ubuntu 14.04 server. We will assume that ODL and OpenStack are already installed and show the steps to enable their integration.

Installing OpenDaylight features

As mentioned in previous chapters, OpenDaylight has the ability to install only specific features that are needed for implementing a software-defined network. For integration with OpenStack, ODL needs to support OVSDB protocol and Neutron API request processing features. The following steps show how to enable support for these features in ODL:

1. Follow the steps shown in `Chapter 5`, *Getting Started with OpenDaylight*, to install ODL.

2. Run the `karaf` command of OpenDaylight, as shown in the following screenshot:

```
openstack@openstack-base:~/distribution-karaf-0.4.2-Beryllium-SR2$ ./bin/karaf
OpenJDK 64-Bit Server VM warning: ignoring option MaxPermSize=512m; support was removed in 8.0




Hit '<tab>' for a list of available commands
and '[cmd] --help' for help on a specific command.
Hit '<ctrl-d>' or type 'system:shutdown' or 'logout' to shutdown OpenDaylight.

opendaylight-user@root>
```

3. Install the ODL OVSDB OpenStack feature, as shown in the following screenshot:

```
opendaylight-user@root>
opendaylight-user@root>feature:install odl-ovsdb-openstack
opendaylight-user@root>
```

4. Due to some race conditions related to the ODL configuration process, it is recommended to wait for 30 to 40 seconds. This is because the installation process may continue in the background even though the main screen shows that the command has completed.

5. Use the `feature:install` command to install the L2 switch package, as shown in the following screenshot:

```
opendaylight-user@root>
opendaylight-user@root> feature:install odl-l2switch-all
opendaylight-user@root>
```

6. Once again, wait for 30 to 40 seconds, and then install the DLUX package, as shown in the following screenshot:

```
opendaylight-user@root>feature:install odl-dlux-all
opendaylight-user@root>
```

7. In order to verify that the features are installed, we will execute an HTTP GET request on ODL, as shown in the following screenshot. Replace the IP address of the HTTP request with the IP address of your ODL server:

```
odlnode:~ odl$ curl -u admin:admin http://192.168.1.120:8080/controller/nb/v2/neutron/networks
{
    "networks" : [ ]
}
odlnode:~ odl$
odlnode:~ odl$
```

8. The HTTP GET command reports an empty list of networks. This means that the features have been installed successfully.

We can also check if the ODL GUI has been installed as shown in Chapter 5, *Getting started with OpenDaylight*. At this time, ODL is ready to process incoming networking requests from OpenStack.

Configuring Neutron on the OpenStack controller node

Now let us see the configuration changes needed on the OpenStack controller node in order to integrate with ODL. As mentioned in the previous section, Neutron needs to be configured with the ML2 plugin and ODL driver. This will ensure that network provisioning requests are sent to ODL for further processing:

1. Install ODL and follow the steps given previously to install the ODL features necessary for the integration. Make a note of the IP address of the OpenDaylight controller. We will be using that information in some of the steps while configuring Neutron.

2. On the OpenStack controller node, shut down the neutron-server process, as shown here:

```
openstack@openstack:~$ sudo service neutron-server stop
neutron-server stop/waiting
```

3. In *Figure 1*, we can see that the OVS agent configures the OVS bridges locally. As part of the OpenStack-ODL integration, ODL will now directly configure the OVS bridges. Therefore, we do not need the OVS agent. The following commands will stop the OVS agent service and uninstall the corresponding software packages:

```
sudo service neutron-openvswitch-agent stop
```

4. The next step is to clear all the configuration and databases of the earlier OVS instance. The following commands stop the OVS instance and remove all configuration and databases:

```
sudo apt-get purge neutron-openvswitch-agent -y
```

5. We will now configure the OVS system on the controller node to be managed by the ODL platform. The following command will print the UUID of the OVS system:

```
sudo service neutron-openvswitch-agent stop

sudo apt-get purge neutron-openvswitch-agent -y
```

6. Next, we will use the UUID returned by the previous command to configure the VXLAN Tunnel IP address, as shown here:

```
sudo service openvswitch-switch stop
sudo rm -rf /var/log/openvswitch/*
sudo rm -rf /etc/openvswitch/conf.db
sudo service openvswitch-switch start
```

7. The following command ensures that the OpenDaylight server will manage the Open vSwitch system on the controller node:

```
sudo ovs-vsctl get Open_vSwitch . _uuid
```

8. Now we will configure the Neutron to use OpenDaylight Neutron driver. We will start with the installation of ODL Neutron driver packages, as shown here:

```
ovs-vsctl set Open_vSwitch <UUID> other_config={local_ip=<Tunnel_IP_address>}
```

9. Open the Neutron ML2 configuration file located at `/etc/neutron/plugins/ml2/ml2_conf.ini` and configure the `[ml2]` section, as shown in the following screenshot:

```
ovs-vsctl set-manager tcp:<ODL_Server_IP>:6640
```

10. Continue editing the Neutron ML2 configuration file and ensure that the `[ml2_odl]` is configured as shown in the following screenshot. The IP address in the ODL URL may change, depending on your setup:

```
sudo apt-get install python-networking-odl -y
```

11. Start the Neutron server using the following command:

```
sudo service neutron-server start
```

The preceding steps complete the procedure to configure Neutron on the controller nodes for OpenDaylight integration.

Configuring Neutron on the compute node(s)

The compute nodes in OpenStack do not run the Neutron server process. Therefore, on the compute node, you must execute steps 3 to 7 only.

Verifying the complete setup

As seen in the previous section, there are several configuration steps to ensure that OpenStack and OpenDaylight work together to provide an SDN-based cloud. Let us now look at some operations that will help us verify if the whole setup is configured correctly:

1. We can verify whether ODL is able to process a Neutron request by executing a simple REST query (HTTP GET operation). The following command tries to fetch all the networks currently managed by OpenDaylight. At this time, since we do not have any OpenStack Networks created, the response for the REST query will be an empty list of networks:

```
[ml2]
type_drivers = flat,vxlan
tenant_network_types = vxlan
mechanism_drivers = opendaylight
extension_drivers = port_security
```

2. We will log into the ODL GUI to confirm that both controller and compute node OVS instances are being managed by ODL. First, we will create a Neutron network and subnet using the OpenStack GUI. Upon successful creation, you should see the following in OpenStack Horizon:

```
[ml2_odl]
username = admin
password = admin
url = http://192.168.1.120:8080/controller/nb/v2/neutron
```

3. We will execute the REST query mentioned in step *1* again. This time, ODL will include the network and the subnet in its response, indicating that the network/subnet create request from OpenStack (Neutron) was indeed processed by ODL:

```
curl -u admin:admin http://<ODL_Server_IP>:8080/controller/nb/v2/neutron/networks
```

4. Since we have configured Neutron to create VXLAN-based networks, the preceding step will result in the establishment of a VXLAN tunnel between Open vSwitches. We can verify this by logging into the ODL GUI. In the following screenshot, one OVS resides on the controller, while the other OVS is created on a compute node. The line connecting the two Open vSwitch instances represents the VXLAN tunnel:

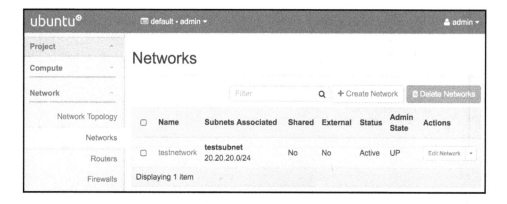

5. The steps so far confirm that Open vSwitch instances on the OpenStack nodes are being managed by OpenDaylight. We can also see that operations performed on OpenStack Neutron result in the OVS being programmed by the ODL directly, without the presence of any agents.

6. Let us look at the final but most critical verification step for the OpenStack-OpenDaylight integration. We will create a virtual machine instance using OpenStack and assign it the network created in Step 2. If the whole integration was configured properly and works, we will find that the VM instance running on the compute nodes gets an IP Address from the DHCP server running on the controller node.

7. We can verify that `tap` interfaces are created in both of the controller and compute nodes necessary for DHCP server and VM connectivity. Use the `ovs-vsctl` command to view the `tap` interfaces on the OVS. The output shown in the following screenshot is for the controller node, therefore the tap interface corresponds to the DHCP server connectivity to the OVS instance:

```
$ curl -u admin:admin http://<ODL_Server_IP>:8080/controller/nb/v2/neutron/networks
{
    "networks" : [ {
        "id" : "02c16e30-4e0c-4d28-9fed-c36b4e0ec146",
        "tenant_id" : "c8cc2a6aff834966867bc553ab92b464",
        "name" : "testnetwork",
        "admin_state_up" : true,
        "shared" : false,
        "router:external" : false,
        "provider:network_type" : "vxlan",
        "provider:segmentation_id" : "99",
        "status" : "ACTIVE",
        "segments" : [ ]
    } ]
}

$ curl -u admin:admin http://<ODL_Server_IP>:8080/controller/nb/v2/neutron/subnets
{
    "subnets" : [ {
        "id" : "97200b80-7f70-4bc7-8fa9-7fee917a0725",
        "tenant_id" : "c8cc2a6aff834966867bc553ab92b464",
        "network_id" : "02c16e30-4e0c-4d28-9fed-c36b4e0ec146",
        "name" : "testsubnet",
        "ip_version" : 4,
        "cidr" : "20.20.20.0/24",
        "gateway_ip" : "20.20.20.1",
        "dns_nameservers" : [ ],
        "allocation_pools" : [ {
            "start" : "20.20.20.2",
            "end" : "20.20.20.254"
        } ],
        "host_routes" : [ ],
        "enable_dhcp" : true,
        "ipv6_address_mode" : null,
        "ipv6_ra_mode" : null
    } ]
}
```

8. Finally, once the VM boots up, we can use the VNC console to check if the VM received a DHCP IP address or not. The following screenshot highlights that the VM got configured with the IP address 20.20.20.3, which was part of the subnet previously created in Step 2. We can also see that the ping command to the DHCP server IP (20.20.20.2) was also successful:

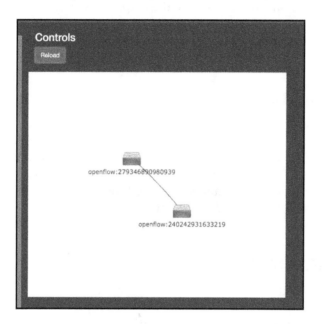

As seen in this section, we need to add features to OpenDaylight to enable integration with OpenStack. We also need to configure OpenStack Neutron to make sure that ODL is processing all the network provisioning requests. Finally, we showed how to verify if the integration is working as expected.

Introduction to Virtual Tenant Network (VTN)

Virtual Tenant Networking (**VTN**), solves two important challenges in software-defined networking. These are multi-tenancy and service chaining. Let us first understand what these challenges are. Then we will see how VTN solves these problems.

Multi-tenancy

One of the key concepts in OpenStack, or for that matter, any cloud infrastructure platform, is multi-tenancy. The definition of tenants varies based on the usage of cloud. Tenants could be organizations that allow one or more employees to make use of cloud platforms. While such an organization is considered a tenant, the employees are called `users`. For privacy and security reasons, it is important to isolate the data traffic of one tenant from another. Therefore, traffic isolation is a key element of cloud and software-defined networking.

Virtualizing the network

The physical networking devices are basically connected using wires. These devices provide specific functionality such as switching, routing and security, and so on. The networking devices connect physical servers. Therefore, applications hosted on these servers directly leverage the underlying *fixed* network connectivity. With the advent of cloud computing, there is a firm trend of applications and servers getting virtualized. As a consequence, networks are also getting virtualized, and software defined.

Service chaining

In a cloud environment, the physical infrastructure, namely, the servers, storage, and networking, is shared by multiple tenants. As mentioned previously, physical networking infrastructure is wired in a specific manner. But different applications belonging to different tenants may require completely different networking capabilities. Service chaining is the mechanism by which software-based networking functions (VNF) are stitched to provide powerful networking constructs for applications. Moreover, these software networking capabilities are expected to leverage the underlying fixed physical networks. This ensures that different tenants can leverage the same shared hardware but are able to define and build their own software-defined networks.

Let us understand this with the help of an example. In traditional networks, traffic originates from a server and passes through one or more switches into a router or firewall device. On the physical firewall device, the network traffic is subjected to multiple security functions, such as firewall, VPN, IDP, anti-virus, and so on. Therefore, the flow of traffic is highly static due to the fixed nature of network traffic. As the network traffic scales, the need to deploy more firewall appliance increases, adding to the total cost of operating the network. The security functions are mostly software applications and can run very well on standard server-class machines.

As modern data centers evolved and cloud became popular, there was an increased need to use the server compute capacity to run these specialized network functions. For example, if there is a need to apply more anti-virus checks, it is possible to *auto scale* only the anti-virus software function *on-demand*. This network architecture is needed for large-scale data centers and cloud. These software-based networking functions are also called **Virtual Network Function (VNF)**.

But this is just a part of the solution. As more VNFs are deployed, it is important to ensure that traffic from one VM instance is appropriately sent to its corresponding VNF for processing. And the processed traffic may have to be sent to yet another VNF handling a different function. This ability to *direct* network traffic through a series of VNF is called **service chaining**.

OpenDaylight Virtual Tenant Network

VTN is an OpenDaylight feature that supports multi-tenancy as well as the chaining of network services. It introduces several networking constructs inside ODL that place power and flexibility at the hand of the end user. This allows end users to define any complex networking required for their applications using software. And as a controller, ODL implements software-defined networks on fixed physical networking hardware.

VTN comprises two components:

- **VTN Manager**: This is an ODL module that implements a multi-tenant virtual network model. It also provides REST API and OpenStack Neutron integration support.
- **VTN Coordinator**: This, on the other hand, is an optional third-party software that is run outside OpenDaylight. As the name suggests, **VTN Coordinator** can talk to more than one **VTN Manager** or ODL instance:

```
$ sudo ovs-vsctl show

f0620005-dd57-493d-80ca-bf974c896800
    Manager "tcp:192.168.56.105:6640"
        is_connected: true
    Bridge br-int
        Controller "tcp:192.168.56.105:6653"
            is_connected: true
        fail_mode: secure
        Port "tapdc672f63-f8"
            Interface "tapdc672f63-f8"
                type: internal
        Port br-int
            Interface br-int
                type: internal
        Port "eth1"
            Interface "eth1"
    ovs_version: "2.5.0"
```

From an OpenStack perspective, we need to focus only on VTN Manager, since it supports integration with Neutron. In the following sections, we will show the mapping of OpenStack Networking entities to the corresponding VTN objects.

VTN model

As mentioned previously, VTN uses a specific object model to implement a multi-tenant virtual network. The model provides a logical abstraction, which allows users to define different types of virtual networks depending on their need. The VTN model can then be mapped to the underlying physical infrastructure and provide real networking connectivity.

The VTN model can be broadly classified into three types of entities. These are as follows:

- VTN nodes:
  - **vBridge**: The vBridge represents a logical Layer 2 switching domain.
  - **vRouter**: The vRouter represents a Layer 3 router, which can connect more than one vBridge.
- VTN interfaces:
  - **vInterface**: These are virtual network ports that reside on the VTN nodes. They represent traffic entry and exit points in most implementations.
- VTN links:
  - **vLink**: The vLink represents the *connectivity* between two VTN interfaces.

These are the most important entities that make up the VTN model. As mentioned previously, users can create a complete network model using these entities in OpenDaylight. Once a virtual network model is defined, the next step is to provide mapping.

Mapping is provided by associating the vInterfaces to interfaces on the physical networks. Since multi-tenancy is a requirement, it is common to map more than one vInterface to the same physical network port. However, in this case, the mapping must also define how the isolation of traffic needs to happen on the physical port.

Let us understand modeling and the mapping process with the help of a simple example.

The setup shown in the following diagram has two servers, each containing two virtual machines. The servers are connected to the physical switch at ports **PIF1** and **PIF2**:

```
                Connected (unencrypted) to: QEMU (instance-00000002)
$ ping 20.20.20.2
PING 20.20.20.2 (20.20.20.2): 56 data bytes
64 bytes from 20.20.20.2: seq=0 ttl=64 time=3.169 ms
64 bytes from 20.20.20.2: seq=1 ttl=64 time=3.081 ms

--- 20.20.20.2 ping statistics ---
2 packets transmitted, 2 packets received, 0% packet loss
round-trip min/avg/max = 3.081/3.125/3.169 ms
$ ifconfig eth0
eth0      Link encap:Ethernet  HWaddr FA:16:3E:C1:F5:DE
          inet addr:20.20.20.3  Bcast:20.20.20.255  Mask:255.255.255.0
          inet6 addr: fe80::f016:3eff:fec1:f5de/64 Scope:Link
          UP BROADCAST RUNNING MULTICAST  MTU:1450  Metric:1
          RX packets:90 errors:0 dropped:2 overruns:0 frame:0
          TX packets:125 errors:0 dropped:0 overruns:0 carrier:0
          collisions:0 txqueuelen:1000
          RX bytes:9416 (9.1 KiB)  TX bytes:11816 (11.5 KiB)

$
```

Mapping of physical layer resources to VTN model

In terms of virtual network, the virtual machines belong to two different tenants. This is represented using **VTN Blue** and **VTN Green** respectively. The corresponding VTN model consists of two vBridge entities, each with two vInterfaces, **VIF1** and **VIF2**.

Once the model is defined, it is important to map the virtual interfaces to the physical interfaces. Since the physical interface on the switch is common to both virtual networks, we will have to use isolation mechanisms, such as VLAN. So a simple VLAN-based mapping could be as follows:

Bridge name	VIF name	PIF name	VLAN ID	VM name
vBridge1	VIF1	PIF1	100	VM1
vBridge 1	VIF2	PIF2	100	VM3
vBridge 2	VIF1	PIF1	200	VM2
vBridge 2	VIF2	PIF2	200	VM4

Installing VTN manager

So far, we have seen a high-level overview of VTN concepts in OpenDaylight. Let us now get a more hands-on understanding of VTN and how the models and mappings are realized in an OpenStack environment.

The first step is to install VTN manager features in ODL. At the ODL Karaf prompt, execute the commands shown here to install VTN manager:

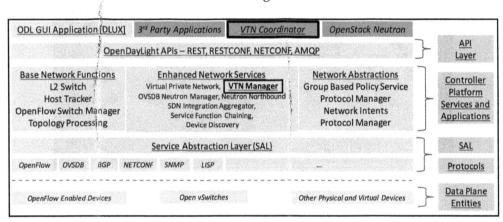

The preceding steps integrate Neutron support for VTN. Once the `odl-vtn-manager-neutron` module is installed, ODL is able to convert OpenStack Networking entities such as network, port, and so on, into corresponding VTN objects.

VTN and OpenStack

As seen previously, for the practical implementation of SDN-based clouds, it is important that ODL and OpenStack integrate seamlessly with each other. We have already shown how OpenStack Neutron integrates with ODL. We will now take this integration further by showing how VTN features of ODL integrate with OpenStack.

Users of OpenStack are highly likely to use only an OpenStack interface (CLI or GUI) to provision workloads in the cloud. This implies that even network provisioning is performed using OpenStack. The most important entities in OpenStack Networking are network, port for Layer 2 connectivity, and router for Layer 3 connectivity. Using a plugin or driver-based approach, OpenStack allows third-party applications to configure the physical and virtual network for these entities.

VTN to OpenStack entity mapping

As seen in the preceding section, ODL acts as a mechanism driver in OpenStack Neutron and takes on the responsibility of providing OVS instances. With the help of VTN, ODL can provide a more complete networking solution by creating common abstractions for virtual and physical networking. Let us now see how OpenStack Networking entities map to a VTN object model:

OpenStack entity	VTN object	Description
Tenant	VTN	In OpenStack, networks are specific to each tenant. This is required to define the boundaries between two networks. Since tenant is the encompassing entity, each tenant is assigned a VTN inside ODL. The name of the VTN is mapped to the UUID of OpenStack tenant.
Network	vBridge	Network in OpenStack represents the logical Layer 2 switching domain. This naturally maps to a vBridge in VTN. OpenStack allows multiple Networks to be created by a tenant. This would result in multiple vBridges, which continue to be isolated from each other.
Router	vRouter	Router in OpenStack and vRouter in VTN represent the Layer 3 routing domain. An OpenStack router connects two or more networks and the VTN vRouter connects two or more vBridges.
Port	vInterface	Finally, as discussed previously, vInterface represent the ingress and egress points for data traffic. This maps very accurately to Ports in OpenStack.

Let us use a real OpenStack example and see how these mappings are implemented in VTN. In the previous chapter, we showed how to set up OpenStack and ODL integration. We will use the same setup for the following steps:

1. The setup contains multiple tenants. We can use the OpenStack CLI to view the name and the ID for each tenant, as shown in the following screenshot:

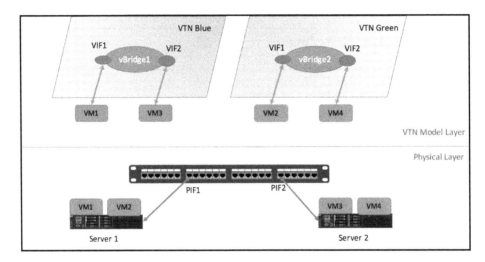

2. We will now execute a REST GET command to fetch all VTNs in the ODL. We will use the curl command, as shown in the following screenshot, to get all VTN objects:

```
opendaylight-user@root>feature:install odl-vtn-manager

opendaylight-user@root>feature:install odl-vtn-manager-neutron

opendaylight-user@root>feature:install odl-vtn-manager-rest
```

3. The output JSON data can be formatted to show that there are two VTN objects. Notice that the name of each VTN object matches the ID of the OpenStack tenants, namely, Admin and Demo:

```
openstack@openstack:~$ openstack project list
+----------------------------------+---------+
| ID                               | Name    |
+----------------------------------+---------+
| 257fd05663844a1f8e04cfd839434754 | admin   |
| 58668a6314cd424da1bc1e94c161eef9 | service |
| 635a42bde92b443285f242078dc5156c | demo    |
+----------------------------------+---------+
openstack@openstack:~$
```

4. Let us now execute the OpenStack command to list all networks. We have three OpenStack Networks, as shown in the following screenshot:

```
curl --user "admin":"admin" -H "Content-type: application/json" \
    -X GET http://192.168.1.120:8181/restconf/operational/vtn:vtns/
```

5. Let us execute the `curl` command shown previously to fetch the VTN objects. If we format the JSON output appropriately, we can see that for the VTN name `257fd0566384a1f8e04cfd839434754`, there are two vBridge objects. This maps to the two networks belonging to the `Admin` tenant:

```
{
  "vtns": {
    "vtn": [
      {
        "name": "257fd0566384a1f8e04cfd839434754",
        "vtenant-config": {...},
        "vbridge": [...]
      },
      {
        "name": "635a42bde92b43285f242078dc5156c",
        "vtenant-config": {...},
        "vbridge": [
          {...}
        ]
      }
    ]
  }
}
```

The output of the GET command for all VTN contains further details, such as `vinterface` and so on. Since an OpenStack Network creation automatically creates a DHCP server and port, we see `vinterface` objects on the VTN mapping for the same.

Summary

OpenDaylight is an SDN controller which, along with OpenStack, can provide cloud users with flexible software-defined networks. In this chapter, we described the components involved in OpenStack and OpenDaylight integration. We showed the steps involved in setting up and configuring OpenDaylight as a Neutron driver in OpenStack. We introduced Virtual Tenant Network (VTN) functionality in ODL and explored how VTN solves some important problems in cloud networking. In the following two chapters, we will cover OpenContrail, which is a popular and competing SDN technology. Similar to ODL, we will cover the architecture, OpenStack integration, and other features of OpenContrail.

7
Getting Started with OpenContrail

In Chapter 5, *Getting Started with OpenDaylight*, we introduced OpenDaylight as an open source SDN controller that leverages OpenFlow protocol and Open vSwitch to provide a feature-rich SDN solution. In Chapter 6, *Using OpenDaylight with OpenStack*, we showed how ODL integrates with OpenStack and solves some key cloud-networking problems.

We will now introduce you to OpenContrail, which is one of the most popular SDN and NFV solutions specifically for OpenStack-based cloud infrastructure. While ODL leverages an independent virtual switch OVS, OpenContrail works with its own virtual networking software, called vRouter.

In this chapter, we will start with an introduction to OpenContrail and then covers its architecture in detail. We will show how to install and use OpenContrail and will conclude the chapter with a quick introduction to using OpenContrail in an OpenStack environment. We will cover the following topics in this chapter:

- Introduction to OpenContrail
- OpenContrail architecture
- Installing OpenContrail
- OpenContrail and OpenStack

Introduction to OpenContrail

OpenContrail is an Apache 2.0 licensed open source project that provides a complete SDN and network virtualization solution for cloud infrastructure. The OpenContrail project architecture addresses networking requirements for two main use cases.

History

OpenContrail can trace its roots to Contrail Systems, a startup focused on disrupting the traditional hardware-oriented networking industry. It created a software-centric networking solution to help drive the need for SDN. In 2012, Contrail Systems was acquired by Juniper Networks and soon thereafter, the software was released under an Apache 2.0 license as an open source project called **OpenContrail**.

Use cases

Increasingly, operators are migrating toward software-based networking functions for firewall, WAN optimizers, load balancers, and intrusion prevention. These networking functions are implemented in software using specific virtual machine appliances instead of physical hardware. These appliances and functions are also known as Virtual Network Functions (VNF). OpenContrail provides orchestration and service chaining capabilities to allow cloud users (tenants) to leverage VNFs and allow them to create their own custom network topology.

The second important use case is that of cloud networking. As enterprises and users adopt private clouds for building and deploying applications, there is a need to provide virtual L2 and L3 connectivity to virtual machines. In addition to traffic isolation between different tenants, it is also important to provide basic security for network traffic. OpenContrail works with cloud platforms like OpenStack (Neutron project) to provide these basic cloud networking capabilities.

OpenContrail architecture

The architecture of OpenContrail can be broken up into two main components:

- vRouter
- Controller

Let us examine each of these components in detail.

vRouter

The vRouter is the main component in the forwarding plane of OpenContrail. The vRouter runs on the Compute Nodes and acts as a virtual switch as well as a virtual router. It forwards the traffic to and from the virtual machines running on the Compute Node. Since OpenContrail is based on an overlay network architecture, the vRouter acts as the endpoint for overlay networks.

The vRouter is analogous to the Open vSwitch (OVS) when compared with an OpenDaylight-based SDN architecture. While OVS supports protocols like OpenFlow to program the forwarding plane, the vRouter uses XMPP as the control plane protocol. **XMPP** stands for **Extensible Messaging and Presence Protocol**. XMPP is an interesting choice for the control plane protocol. XMPP was designed as a protocol for detecting the presence and exchanging messages for real-time communication. While the OpenFlow protocol is intended specifically for control plane messages, XMPP, which is based on XML, is more flexible and versatile. XMPP can be used to exchange control plane and management plane information.

Compute Node components

Let us now see what goes on inside a Compute Node in an OpenContrail-based SDN solution. The following diagram shows the various components that interact with each other on a Compute Node.

As you can see, the vRouter provides network connectivity to virtual machines. The forwarding tables and related information is programmed into the **vRouter kernel module** (vRouter Forwarding Plane) by the **vRouter Agent** running alongside. The **vRouter Agent** is a user-space program, whereas the actual forwarding is done in the kernel module for optimum performance:

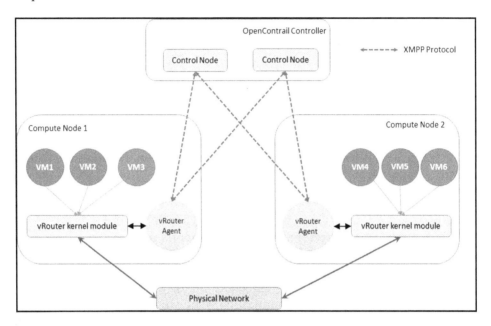

Figure 1: vRouter on a Compute Node

In the preceding diagram, we can also see that all vRouter agents communicate with the centralized OpenContrail controller. The agents and the controller use XMPP as the communication protocol.

The **Control Node** comprises the central control plane, which is an important requirement for any SDN solution. We will cover the Control Nodes in more detail in the section titled *Control Node*.

Functions of vRouter agent

The primary function of a vRouter agent is to process XMPP-based control plane messages from the controller and to program or configure the forwarding information into the vRouter forwarding plane (kernel module). Additionally, the vRouter agent also collects statistics and logs related to network flow and sends them to the controller for analysis and reporting. Finally, in an OpenStack environment, the vRouter agent is responsible for interaction with other OpenStack agents such as the Nova agent for processing OpenStack networking requests.

Functions of vRouter forwarding plane

The obvious function of the vRouter forwarding plane (kernel module) is to forward data packets. OpenContrail use encapsulation to separate the tenant networks (overlays) from the physical networks (underlays). This encapsulation of overlay packets into an underlay packet is performed by the vRouter kernel module. OpenContrail supports MPLS labels or VXLAN VNI to identify overlay network traffic.

Controller

The controller handles the control and management plane functions within the OpenContrail network architecture. The controller itself comprises several other components (known as **nodes**). The controller provides rich REST APIs that can be used by external applications such as OpenStack and third-party OSS/BSS systems. The OpenContrail web interface also uses these REST APIs.

The controller consists of three main components, as shown in *Figure 2*. Let us now see the functions of each node in the OpenContrail controller.

Configuration Node

The **Configuration Node** supports several important functions. These are as follows:

- Processing incoming REST API requests. In the case of OpenContrail, the incoming REST requests are from the web-based GUI and OpenStack Neutron.
- Translating high-level network entities and a state (model) into a low-level model, which can be used for controlling and programming the vRouter and other network devices.
- Interacting with the **Control Node** to provide management of vRouters using the IF-MAP protocol.

- Maintaining and sharing information about the status and reachability of other nodes of the controller.
- The **Configuration Node** can be considered the central entity, which provides the core management capabilities for an OpenContrail-based SDN deployment:

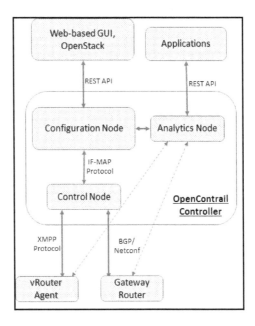

Figure 2: High-level architecture of OpenContrail controller

Control Node

While the Configuration Nodes provide management plane functionality, the Control Nodes handle the centralized control-plane responsibilities. The Control Nodes receive the configuration and network state information from the Configuration Node using the **IF-MAP Protocol**.

The Control Nodes then communicate with the vRouter agents that run on the Compute Nodes using XMPP protocol. The Control Nodes process route information from all vRouters and apply forwarding rules on the vRouter using the XMPP protocol. The Control Nodes can interact with physical routers in the network using BGP or Netconf protocols.

Analytics Node

The **Analytics Node** is also part of the management capabilities supported by OpenContrail. The Analytics Node can receive logs, statistics, and events from vRouters, and even from physical network devices. It ingests this information and performs advanced analysis to present more actionable and meaningful information about the status of the network.

The Analytics Nodes support collectors that use an XML-based protocol to collect statistics and log information. This information is stored in a NoSQL database. The collected information is analyzed and correlated to make it easy for the end user to consume. The summarized information is exposed to applications via REST APIs.

Scalability

OpenContrail was designed to be a highly scalable and robust deployment. Each node can be installed independently and many instances of each node can coexist. Using internal protocols such as Sandesh (messaging), these instances ensure that OpenContrail's distributed architecture can handle the stringent requirements for large-scale cloud networks.

Putting it all together

In the previous sections, we have seen the different components of an OpenContrail-based SDN solution. Let us now put all these components together and understand the overall architecture of OpenContrail. We will also highlight the OpenStack integration points.

Figure 3 shows the complete deployment architecture for OpenContrail. We also show OpenStack nodes in this diagram to highlight the tight integration that OpenContrail has with OpenStack:

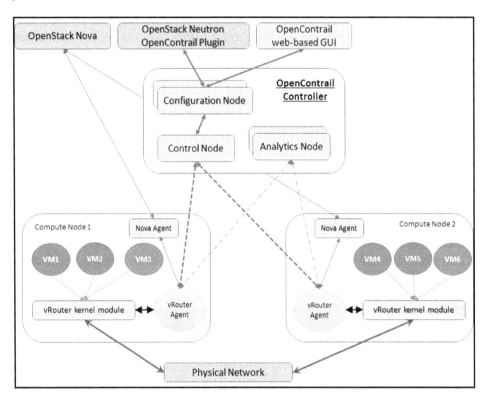

Figure 3: Full deployment architecture

The two Compute Nodes are part of an OpenStack cluster running services such as the **Nova Agent** and so on. In addition, these Compute Nodes also run OpenContrail vRouter components to provision an SDN-based virtual network. We have shown that the **Nova Agent** on the **Compute Node** interacts with the **vRouter Agent**, and will be covering this interaction in a later section.

The OpenStack component's Nova server and Neutron server are also part of the OpenStack cluster of nodes. Typically, these services run on the OpenStack controller node. Note that Neutron is configured with OpenContrail as the *core* plugin. *Figure 3* also shows that OpenContrail REST APIs are used by the Neutron plugin, as well as the OpenContrail web-based GUI.

The OpenContrail controller is a logical collection of several nodes. These nodes could be running the same server or several different physical servers. This usually depends on the scale of the SDN to be supported in a given deployment.

Installing OpenContrail

OpenContrail is available under the Apache 2.0 license as a fully open source project. It is an actively maintained project and the best way to get a feel for OpenContrail is to build and install it from source code.

Version

For the purposes of this section, we will use OpenContrail version 3.0.

Prerequisites

In order to get hands-on knowledge of installing OpenContrail, we will use the Ubuntu Server 14.04.4 LTS-based server or a virtual machine. A minimum of 4 GB RAM (recommended 8 GB) and 70 GB hard disk space is needed for this procedure.

Installing OpenContrail

The OpenContrail project supports different types of installation scripts, including steps to integrate with OpenStack. In this section, we will focus on building and installing OpenContrail from source code on GitHub:

1. The first step is to check out the OpenContrail installer scripts from GitHub. Execute the following command on your Ubuntu shell:

```
openstack@openstack:~$ git clone https://github.com/Juniper/contrail-installer
Cloning into 'contrail-installer'...
remote: Counting objects: 1178, done.
remote: Total 1178 (delta 0), reused 0 (delta 0), pack-reused 1178
Receiving objects: 100% (1178/1178), 2.98 MiB | 107.00 KiB/s, done.
Resolving deltas: 100% (679/679), done.
Checking connectivity... done.
```

2. Use the `cd` command to change the working directory to `contrail-installer`, as shown in the following screenshot:

```
openstack@openstack:~$ ls
contrail-installer
openstack@openstack:~$ cd contrail-installer/
openstack@openstack:~/contrail-installer$ ls
cassandra-env.sh.patch        Contrail_user_guide.txt  localrc       setup_contrail.py
clean.py                      devstack                 log           setup_devstack.sh
contrail                      docs                     README.md     taskrc
contrail_config_functions     functions                README.txt    test_domainlist.py
contrail_config_templates.py  installer.xml            samples       test_network_simple.sh
contrail.sh                   install_pip.sh           service.sh    utilities
openstack@openstack:~/contrail-installer$
```

3. Copy the local settings file from the samples directory, as shown in the following screenshot:

```
openstack@openstack:~/contrail-installer$
openstack@openstack:~/contrail-installer$ cp samples/localrc-all localrc
openstack@openstack:~/contrail-installer$
```

4. Edit the `localrc` if required. The default `localrc` file is configured to use SSH for accessing the `contrail` repository. At the time of writing this book, the configuration parameter was commented out, which meant that SSH would be the protocol to access the `contrail` repository. Edit the `localrc` file using a text editor and ensure that the `CONTRAIL_REPO_PROTO` is set to HTTPS, as shown here:

   CONTRAIL_REPO_PROTO=https

5. The vRouter binds to a specific network interface and depending upon your setup, you may have to configure the attribute `PHYSICAL_INTERFACE` inside the `localrc` file.

6. Now we will build OpenContrail from source code using the command as follows:

   openstack@openstack:~/contrail-installer$ ./contrail.sh build

7. The build step creates all the binaries and packages needed for OpenContrail. The next step is to install these software packages as follows:

   openstack@openstack:~/contrail-installer$ ./contrail.sh install

8. Once the install process completes successfully, the final step is to configure OpenContrail. Use the command as follows:

```
openstack@openstack: ~/contrail-installer$ ./contrail.sh configure
```

9. The final step is to start OpenContrail services using the `contrail.sh` script.

```
openstack@openstack: ~/contrail-installer$ ./contrail.sh start
```

The build, install, and startup script will display error messages if things go wrong during the process. You should be able to refer to OpenContrail documentation to correct the error.

OpenContrail and OpenStack

So far in this chapter, we have presented a high-level view of the OpenContrail architecture. We have also seen how to install and do basic operations with OpenContrail. We will end this chapter with an overview of the integration between OpenStack and OpenContrail. A more hands-on detail of this integration will be shared in the next chapter.

Neutron and Nova integration

Neutron is the networking project within the OpenStack platform. As an SDN platform, it is natural that OpenContrail integrates with OpenStack Neutron using a plugin. Since OpenContrail supports a large set of networking services, it is configured as a *core plugin* in Neutron.

In addition to Neutron, OpenContrail also responds to `port` creation requests from Nova. Once a virtual machine instance is created by Nova, the Nova agent requests the creation of logical ports to provide network connectivity to that virtual machine. This request is sent by the Nova agent to the local vRouter agent on the Compute Node.

High-level flow of requests from OpenStack

Let us now look at the flow of requests from OpenStack and how these operations result in OpenContrail functionalities being invoked. For discussion purposes, we will assume that the user uses the OpenStack web GUI to perform the operations:

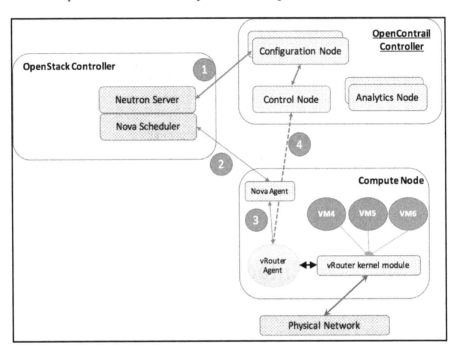

Step by step flow of requests between OpenStack and OpenContrail

The preceding figure shows the step-by-step flow of requests between OpenStack and OpenContrail. Let us now see what happens in each of the steps:

1. In OpenStack, the first operation is usually to create a network. This operation will send a create network request to Neutron. In the case of OpenContrail, the plugin will delegate this call directly to the OpenContrail API and will be processed by the configuration. Depending on the type of virtual network, OpenContrail will allocate some resources for this network. For example, for a VXLAN-based network, a **VXLAN Network Identifier** (**VNI**) will be assigned.

2. Once a virtual network is created for a tenant, the next step is to create a VM instance that attaches to this network. This operation of creating an instance is processed by the Nova service in OpenStack. On the **Compute Node**, the **Nova Agent** processes the request to create a VM instance.

3. This is followed by another call to create and attach the virtual interface of the VM to the user-specified network. This request is also processed by Nova, but the specific virtual interface creation is handled by the OpenContrail driver.
4. The OpenContrail virtual interface driver (for Nova) uses the vRouter API to ensure that the vRouter fetches the correct configuration for this virtual network interface from the controller and uses this configuration to provision the forwarding rules locally inside the **vRouter kernel module**.

Summary

In this chapter, we presented a high-level overview of OpenContrail. The two key components of OpenContrail, namely, the vRouter and controller, and the overall architecture were also covered. We then walked you through a hands-on installation procedure for OpenContrail. Finally, we discussed the high-level interaction between OpenStack and OpenContrail. In the following chapter, we will cover the OpenStack integration in more detail, including hands-on steps. We will also discuss advanced services such as routing and security in the context of OpenContrail.

8
OpenContrail Networking with OpenStack

In Chapter 7, *Getting Started with OpenContrail*, we introduced **OpenContrail** as an open source controller for SDN and NFV implementations. With its own virtual networking element (vRouter) and a powerful architecture, OpenContrail is among the most popular SDN platforms for OpenStack.

We covered an introduction to OpenContrail and OpenStack briefly in the previous chapter. In this chapter, we will go through this integration in more detail. Starting with a step-by-step guide for the integration, we will take you through the basic capabilities of OpenContrail. We will use the OpenContrail GUI and CLI to get a better understanding of the virtual networking capabilities. We will then look at the advanced networking services that can be realized using OpenContrail and OpenStack.

We will cover the following topics in this chapter:

- Integrating OpenContrail with OpenStack
- Virtual network management in OpenContrail
- Data-packet flow in OpenContrail
- Service chaining using OpenContrail

OpenContrail integration with OpenStack

While OpenContrail is a powerful SDN solution by itself, it is designed to work seamlessly with the OpenStack cloud platform. OpenContrail not only integrates with Neutron using a plugin, but it also relies on other OpenStack services, such as **Keystone**, **Glance**, and **Nova**. First, we will show you how to integrate OpenStack with OpenContrail. We will then show you the interaction with various OpenStack services.

DevStack-based installation

In Chapter 7, *Getting Started with OpenContrail*, we showed the steps to install OpenContrail directly from the source code. In order to learn OpenContrail integration with OpenStack, we will use **DevStack** to perform the OpenStack installation and configuration. DevStack is a set of scripts that installs OpenStack for learning, development, and experimentation. It is important to note that DevStack installation will be performed on the same setup where OpenContrail is already installed, as shown in Chapter 7, *Getting Started with OpenContrail*. The following steps show how to install and configure OpenStack for OpenContrail using DevStack:

1. The first step is to check out DevStack from GitHub. In the home directory of your Ubuntu server, execute the git command, as shown here:

   ```
   git clone https://github.com/openstack-dev/devstack -b
   stable/liberty
   ```

2. The next important step is to check and ensure that all OpenContrail services are running properly. We will be using a built-in utility for this. First, we will have to initialize some environment variables, as shown here:

   ```
   export CONTRAIL_DIR=/home/openstack/contrail-installer
   export DEVSTACK_DIR=/home/openstack/devstack
   ```

   We will use the contrail-status utility to check for the status of all the OpenContrail services, as shown in the following screenshot. Ensure that all OpenContrail services' statuses are ACTIVE. If any of the services have any issues, the output will show ERROR against the service and will also display the error details:

```
openstack@openstack:~/contrail-installer$ ./utilities/contrail-status
/home/openstack/contrail-installer
ls: cannot access *.failure: No such file or directory
agent                 : ACTIVE
agent_1               : ACTIVE
analytics-api         : ACTIVE
apiSrv                : ACTIVE
cass                  : ACTIVE
collector             : ACTIVE
control               : ACTIVE
disco                 : ACTIVE
dns                   : ACTIVE
ifmap                 : ACTIVE
named                 : ACTIVE
query-engine          : ACTIVE
redis-w               : ACTIVE
redis                 : ACTIVE
schema                : ACTIVE
svc-mon               : ACTIVE
ui-jobs               : ACTIVE
ui-webs               : ACTIVE
zk                    : ACTIVE
openstack@openstack:~/contrail-installer$
```

3. Now we will proceed with the OpenStack installation using DevStack. The commands shown here will change the directory to the code checked out from GitHub and copy the OpenContrail plugin code to the appropriate folder within DevStack for configuring Neutron:

```
cd devstack
cp ~/contrail-installer/devstack/lib/neutron_plugins/opencontrail lib/neutron_plugins/
```

4. Next, we will create a `localrc` file for DevStack using the samples that come with the OpenContrail installer:

```
cp ~/contrail-installer/devstack/samples/localrc-all localrc
```

5. Add the lines shown here to the `localrc` file using a text editor of your choice. Note that the `SERVICE_HOST` attribute's value may vary based on your setup:

```
disable_service c-sch
disable_service c-api
disable_service c-vol
disable_service tempest

SERVICE_HOST=localhost
```

6. Execute the `stack.sh` program to start the OpenStack installation and configuration process.

By default, DevStack creates an OpenStack account with the username `admin` and a `password` as specified in the `localrc` file, which in our case is `contrail123`. Once the `stack.sh` program completes successfully, you should be able to log into OpenContrail and see the main **Monitor** view of OpenContrail:

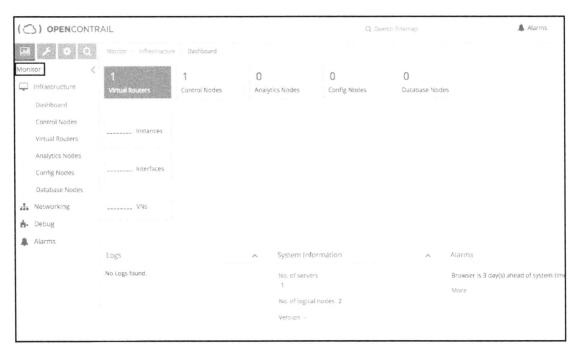

The OpenContrail UI is categorized into four navigation groups. These groups are indicated by the icon on the top navigation bar, as shown in the following screenshot:

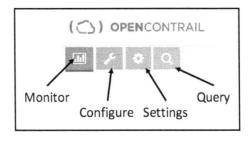

We will be covering the configure-related actions in a bit more detail in the following sections.

OpenStack services used by OpenContrail

We have emphasized that OpenContrail is an SDN platform that integrates closely with cloud orchestration platforms such as OpenStack. Let us now look at the integration in a bit more detail. The following diagram will be used to describe the interaction between OpenStack and OpenContrail components:

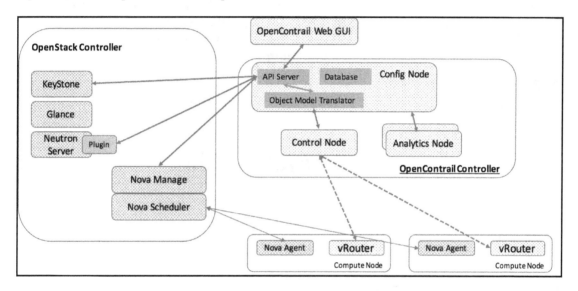

OpenStack services and their interaction with OpenContrail

When we log into OpenContrail, it redirects the authentication requests to the **Keystone** service in OpenStack. In addition to validating the credentials, OpenContrail also uses the user and project information stored in OpenStack to enforce appropriate access control on its user interface.

OpenContrail also communicates with **Glance** for fetching VM images. It is important to note that OpenContrail does not provide capabilities to start arbitrary VM instances. It uses **Glance** to populate and create **Service Templates** and **Service Instances** that allow users to *chain* networking services. We will cover this in detail in the following section.

The integration with Nova addresses two important features in OpenContrail. First, when an end-user VM instance is started, Nova invokes the OpenContrail **Virtual Interface Driver** (**VIF Driver**) to provide connectivity between the VM instance and the vRouter on the compute node. The second aspect of OpenContrail and Nova integration comes into the picture when you create Service Instances in OpenStack. As part of service chaining, virtual network functions are started using Nova APIs.

Finally, the most important and deepest integration between OpenStack and OpenContrail happens with the Neutron service. OpenContrail acts as the *core plugin* for Neutron and thereby handles all the networking API calls made to Neutron. Whether the end user is using the OpenStack GUI or CLI or OpenContrail GUI, all the networking-related requests are processed by OpenContrail. The translation between the OpenStack networking object model (high-level model) to the internal model of OpenContrail is performed by the configuration node within the OpenContrail controller.

All the API requests coming into OpenContrail and the ones made to OpenStack from OpenContrail are processed by an OpenContrail API server process.

Virtual network management in OpenContrail

Let us now take a quick look at the process of creating a virtual network in OpenContrail and how it can be leveraged to provision a VM instance in OpenStack.

Creating virtual networks and VM instances

The steps given here will be important for understanding the service chaining concepts later in this chapter:

1. The first step in creating a **virtual network** (**VN**) is to click on the icon for **Configure** in the OpenContrail navigation bar, as highlighted previously. The following screen should be displayed:

2. Navigate to **Networking | Networks** and click on the + sign on the right-hand side of the screen. This will allow users to create a virtual network in OpenContrail.

3. Enter a name for the VN and in the **Subnets** tab, click on the + sign to add a subnet for this network, as shown in the following screenshot:

4. Once the network creation is successful, you will see the entry in the **Networks** table of OpenContrail, as shown in the following screenshot:

5. We can log into the OpenStack dashboard and navigate to **Project** | **Network** | **Networks**, and confirm that the same VN is listed in OpenStack as well:

The preceding steps show that the OpenStack Neutron APIs have been invoked from OpenContrail. Similarly, it will be easy to check that a network created using the OpenStack GUI is visible inside OpenContrail. As mentioned previously, there is a strong integration between OpenStack Neutron and OpenContrail. From the OpenContrail UI, we can also see that advanced networking service such as routers, floating IPs, security groups, and so on, are also supported as part of this integration.

Monitoring virtual router and virtual networks

In the section titled *Associating a network and subnet to a virtual machine* of Chapter 1, *OpenStack Networking in a Nutshell*, we showed how to create an instance using OpenStack. Once we create an instance, the OpenContrail vRouter and the associated objects come to life.

When a VM instance is created, we are required to select one or more networks. This is required to ensure that there is traffic isolation between VMs belonging to different networks. Internally, this also results in the virtual interface being hooked up to the vRouter infrastructure.

Once a VM is created, the vRouter creates a routing instance specifically for the virtual network that the VM belongs to. A dedicated routing instance means that each virtual network gets its own routing table and forwarding information base to avoid conflicts due to overlapping IP addresses. This routing instance (commonly called **VRF**) is created on the vRouter of the compute node where the instance was created. If another VM on the same virtual network is created on a different compute node, another routing instance will be created.

The virtual interface of the VM instance has a unique MAC address. During the process of VM creation, the MAC address and its IP address are stored in the configuration database of the OpenContrail controller. This MAC address mapping is propagated from the controller to all the compute nodes that have VM instances on the same virtual network. We will elaborate on the use of MAC-address propagation in the following section.

The OpenContrail UI allows management and monitoring of vRouters and the routing instances (VRF) inside each vRouter. In the OpenContrail UI, navigate to **Monitor** | **Infrastructure** | **Virtual Routers** and click on the vRouter **Host name** to view the details of the vRouter:

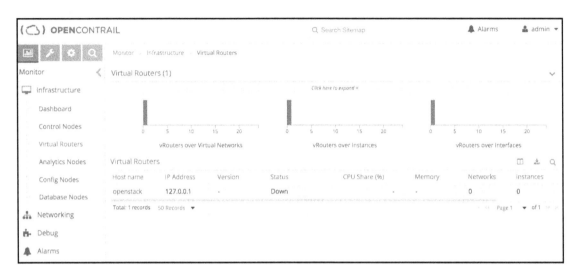

We can see the details of the vRouter, as shown in the following screenshot:

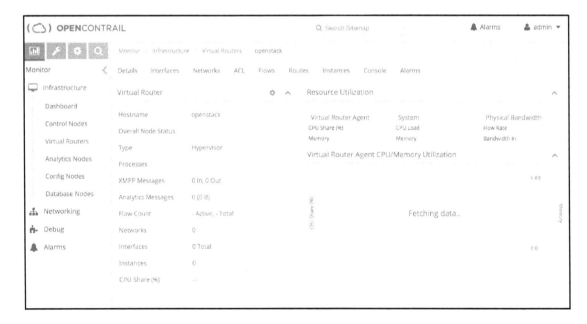

Clicking on Networks will show the list of networks and the associated VRF (routing instances). This list will only show networks that have an instance (and hence a VRF) associated with them:

If we click on the name of the VRF, we should be able to see the routing table-related information, as shown in the following screenshot:

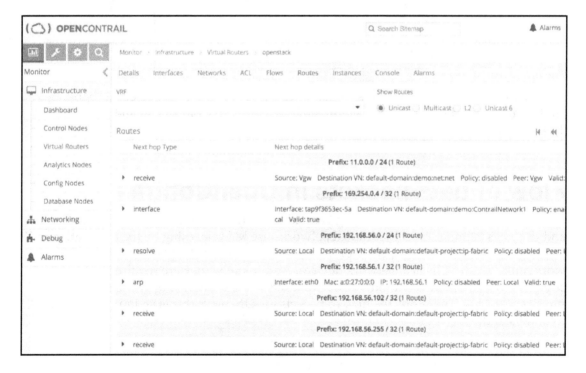

As shown in the preceding screenshot, users can monitor and manage the vRouter and the routing related information from the GUI. OpenContrail also supports a rich introspection interface where much detailed information is available. In order to access the introspection interface, point your browser to `http://<opencontrail_ip>:8085` to show the modules of the vRouter:

Modules for contrail-vrouter-agent

agent.xml
agent_profile.xml
agent_stats_interval.xml
cfg.xml
controller.xml
cpuinfo.xml
diag.xml
discovery_client_stats.xml
flow_stats.xml
ifmap_agent.xml
kstate.xml
multicast.xml
pkt.xml
port_ipc.xml
sandesh_trace.xml
sandesh_uve.xml
services.xml
stats.xml
stats_interval.xml
task.xml
xmpp_server.xml

While a full coverage of each introspection interface is beyond the scope of this book, readers are advised to explore the **agent.xml** link and search for `ItfReq` and `VrfListReq` sub-interfaces.

Flow of data packets in OpenContrail

For proper flow of data packets through any IP network, the learning of MAC addresses and IP routes is imperative. Traditional networks use MAC learning on the data path and IP routes are exchanged using specific protocols. Most modern SDN platforms are designed to work multi-vendor physical network devices. Additionally, they are required at times to support virtual networks without the data packets being examined by the underlying physical network. Therefore, the flow of packets in SDN platforms is an important concept to understand.

Traffic isolation using encapsulation

Overlay network traffic (between VM instances of the same virtual network) is encapsulated and carried across the cloud network. This is needed to provide isolation between different tenant networks.

OpenContrail supports the following encapsulation methods:

- MPLS over GRE
- VXLAN
- MPLS over UDP

We will cover MPLS over GRE in a bit more detail, since that is the default setting for OpenContrail. Moreover, we have covered VXLAN-based overlays in the Open vSwitch-related chapters.

In the case of MPLS over GRE, each VM instance is assigned an MPLS label and this label is propagated to the VRFs participating in that virtual network. The MPLS label of destination VM is prefixed to the IP packets and the whole frame is encapsulated using GRE.

Since OpenContrail is a controller-based SDN solution, the controller is responsible for distributing control plane information to all vRouters. When a VM instance is created on a given virtual network, it is assigned a MAC address (per virtual interface), an IP address, and an MPLS label. As soon as the next VM is created on the same virtual network *but on a different compute node*, the controller ensures that MAC, IP, and MPLS labels of both the VM instances are programmed into the respective VRFs. This information is used by the local vRouter to configure the global routing tables and establish GRE tunnels between the two compute nodes.

As shown previously, we can view the routes that are part of a VRF. We can drill down to view the details of a specific `tap` interface or VM instance's virtual interface to view the MPLS label assigned, and the next-hop information, as shown in the following screenshot:

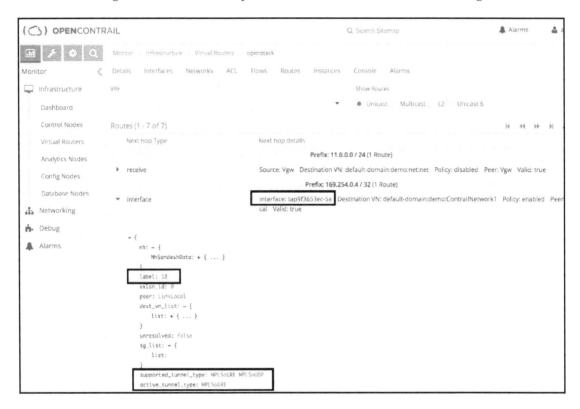

More detailed information can be obtained by looking at the introspection interface. Point your browser to `http://<opencontrail_ip>:8085/Snh_ItfReq`.

Flow of packets in OpenContrail

To illustrate how data packets flow from one VM to another in the case of MPLS over GRE, we will use the following figure. Since we have only a DevStack setup (with one compute node), the following setup has two different OpenStack networks, called **ContrailNetwork1** and **ContrailNetwork2**, connected to each other using an OpenStack router called **ContrailRouter**:

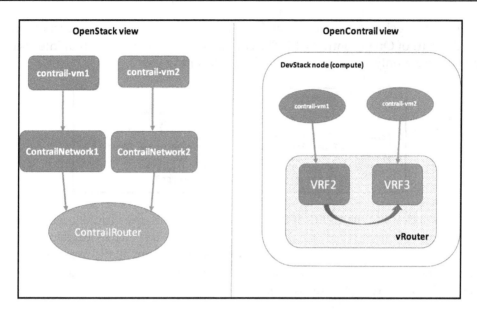

Comparison of the virtual networks in OpenStack versus OpenContrail

On the OpenContrail side, each network is assigned a specific VRF by the vRouter. The listing of Ports in OpenContrail shows the UUID and the IP addresses that will be used for showing packet flow:

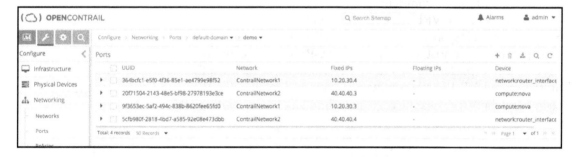

Let us say that VM1 (**10.20.30.3**) wants to send an IP packet to VM2 (**40.40.40.3**). The VM will create an IP packet with the destination of VM2. This IP packet is sent out from the virtual interface (*tap interface*) to the VRF assigned to this VM.

We can check this using the `vif` command, as shown in the following screenshot. The `vif` command is part of OpenContrail CLI. The command will list all the virtual interfaces, but for brevity, we are only showing the one that is relevant to us:

```
openstack@openstack:~$ sudo vif --list
. . .
. . .

vif0/4        OS: tap9f3653ec-5a
              Type:Virtual HWaddr:00:00:5e:00:01:00 IPaddr:0
              Vrf:2 Flags:PL3L2D MTU:9160 QOS:-1 Ref:5
              RX packets:113  bytes:10270 errors:0
              TX packets:78  bytes:7122 errors:0
```

You will also notice that the UUID of the port associated with the virtual interface is used as the suffix for the tap name (`tap9f3653ec-5a`). Notice that the VRF associated with this interface is number 2. Let us now use the `rt` command to dump all the routes in this VRF. The truncated output of the `rt` command shows the *next-hop* information in order to reach the other VM's IP address (`40.40.40.3`):

```
openstack@openstack:~$ sudo rt --dump 2
. . .
. . .
40.40.40.3/32        32        P        -        24        -
```

The full output of the command shows us that the number 24 is the next-hop MPLS label. That means that the VRF will add this label to the IP packet and send the packet further. Since we are using only one host, the packet does not enter the GRE tunnel. If the other VM was on a different host, the appropriate GRE tunnel ID would have been prepended to the MPLS-labeled packet. In this case, the vRouter will forward the MPLS packet to the appropriate VRF. We can use the `nh` command to view the VRF that has the label of 24. As seen here, the VRF3 has the corresponding label in its routing table:

```
openstack@openstack:~$ sudo nh --get 24
Id:24        Type:Encap       Fmly: AF_INET  Rid:0  Ref_cnt:5        Vrf:3
             Flags:Valid, Policy,
             EncapFmly:0806 Oif:5 Len:14
             Encap Data: 02 20 f7 15 04 21 00 00 5e 00 01 00 08 00
```

The VRF3 will remove the MPLS label and send the IP packet to the appropriate destination. The output of the command also shows which *output interface* (Oif) will be used to send the IP packet. As seen in the preceding screenshot, the output interface 5 is used to send the IP packet. Let us now use the vif command once again and see which interface it corresponds to:

```
openstack@openstack:~$ sudo vif --get 5
Vrouter Interface Table

Flags: P=Policy, X=Cross Connect, S=Service Chain, Mr=Receive Mirror
       Mt=Transmit Mirror, Tc=Transmit Checksum Offload, L3=Layer 3, L2=Layer 2
       D=DHCP, Vp=Vhost Physical, Pr=Promiscuous, Vnt=Native Vlan Tagged
       Mnp=No MAC Proxy, Dpdk=DPDK PMD Interface, Rfl=Receive Filtering Offload,
Mon=Interface is Monitored
       Uuf=Unknown Unicast Flood, Vof=VLAN insert/strip offload, Df=Drop New Flows

vif0/5     OS: tap20f71504-21
           Type:Virtual HWaddr:00:00:5e:00:01:00 IPaddr:0
           Vrf:3 Flags:PL3L2D MTU:9160 QOS:-1 Ref:5
           RX packets:50  bytes:4749 errors:0
           TX packets:49  bytes:4946 errors:0
```

If you notice the tap interface name, you will see that it corresponds to the destination VM's port. This means that the IP packet has been forwarded correctly to the destination.

This was a simple example to explain the process of packet forwarding within OpenContrail and also a brief tutorial on the important CLI commands that are part of the platform. In a real-world deployment, the encapsulated overlay network packet travels through the underlay network, which adds its own complexity. That topic is beyond the scope of this discussion on OpenContrail.

Service chaining using OpenContrail

Just as applications migrated from physical servers to VMs, network functions are moving from dedicated hardware to VMs. In order to provide rich networking for virtualized applications, it is important that SDN solutions support the ability to redirect application traffic through different network functions such as firewalls, DPI, load balancers, and so on. This ability of the SDN platform is referred to as service chaining and the specialized network functions are referred to as service instances.

Advanced network services such as firewalls, IDP, load balancers, and so on, usually operate at L4 to L7 of the networking stack. This means that an L3-based overlay network is well suited to support chaining since OpenContrail takes care of L3 packet forwarding. Service chaining in OpenContrail mostly deals with *traffic steering*, which is the ability to force network traffic in a well-defined and controlled manner so that the traffic flows can be processed by Service Instances.

MPLS as a technology supports a predefined path for IP packets to travel through the network. The MPLS **Label Switched Path** (**LSP**) is very useful in service chaining, where labels and routes can be programmed at different vRouters and VRF, such that traffic is *engineered* in and out of various VM instances that are part of the service chain. Competing SDN platforms such as OpenDayLight have to rely on physical network hardware to provide this level of traffic steering, which is neither practical nor flexible when it comes to large-scale cloud networks.

OpenContrail creates special routing instances for the Service Instances, allowing them to insert themselves transparently into the network path between two VMs. They do this by advertising themselves as the next hop for the traffic originating from a VM and also creating a new MPLS label for themselves.

We will now take a simple example and walk you through the service chaining workflow in the OpenContrail GUI. The goal of this exercise is to show a service chain where VMs from two different networks are connected by a virtual firewall, as shown here:

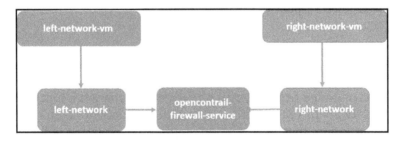

Components used for service chaining example

The first thing we need to accomplish this service chain is to create an image in OpenStack Glance that corresponds to a firewall VM. For the purpose of this chapter, we have created an image named `demo-firewall-image-cirros` using a standard Cirros image. For real deployments, you must use an appropriate NFV appliance:

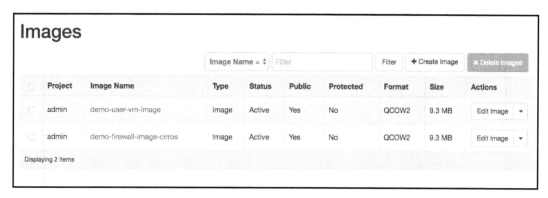

Next, we will go ahead and create the two virtual networks and provision one end-user VM in each of the virtual networks. Once configured, you can see the **Ports** table in OpenContrail to confirm the setup:

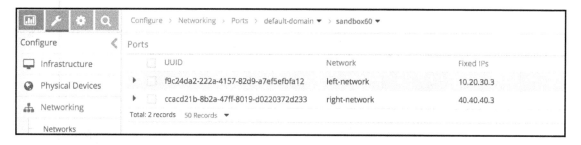

The first important step in the creation of service chaining is to create a service chain template. In the OpenContrail UI, navigate to **Configure** | **Services** | **Service Templates** and click on the + sign on the right-hand side. This will result in the **Create Service Template** form being displayed:

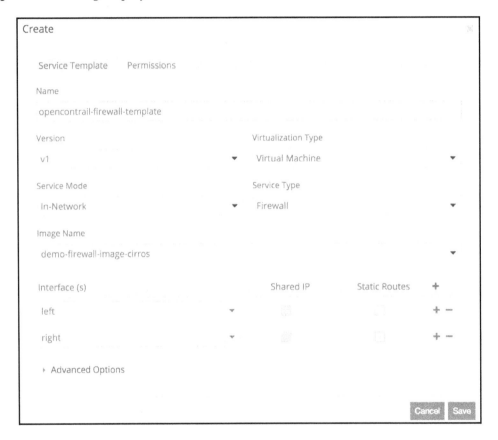

Enter an appropriate **Name** for the template and select the **Version** as v1 and **Service Mode** to be **In-Network**. We will choose the **demo-firewall-image-cirros** as the image for the service VM. Since we are creating a simple linear service chain, we will have to select at least two interfaces for this service VM, **left** and **right**. In a real deployment, it is common to have another interface, called *management*, to help the user manage the virtual network function (service). Click on **Save** to save the template.

The next step is to create an instance of the service using the template. In the OpenContrail UI, navigate to **Configure** | **Services** | **Service Instance** and click on the + sign on the right. This action will display the **Create Service Instance** form, as shown in the following screenshot:

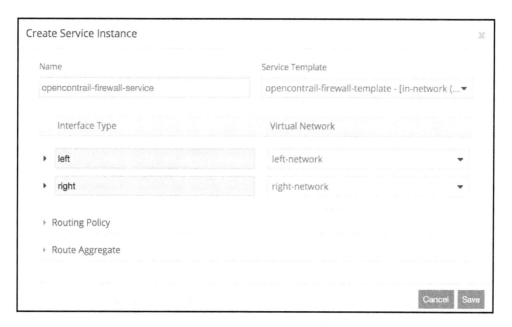

Once again, enter a name for the instance and then select the correct service template for this instance. The next step is very important, assigning the virtual networks to the interfaces of the service instance. To match our initial deployment diagram, we will assign **left-network** to the **left** interface of the service instance. Similarly, we will add the **right** interface for the instance. Upon clicking **Save**, OpenContrail will attempt to spawn the VM instance using Nova APIs.

Once the service instance is launched, we can view its details using the OpenStack UI as shown in the following screenshot:

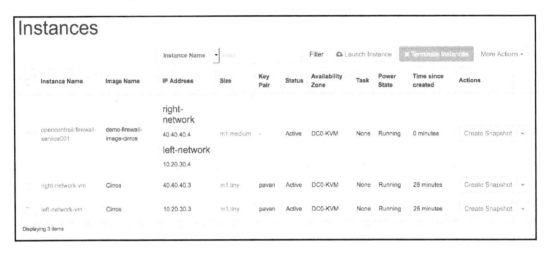

We can also see how the virtual network topology changes before and after the service creation:

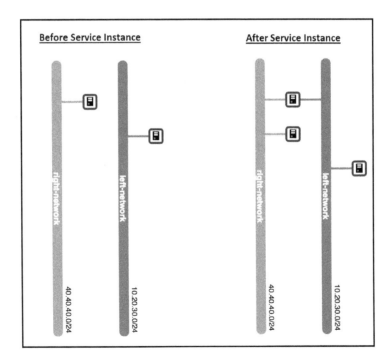

We can see that the firewall service instance is now attached to both networks. OpenContrail will have programmed the routing instances such that traffic from either network passes through the service VM.

We can also use the OpenContrail UI to configure fine-grained policies on this service VM. Navigate to **Configure** | **Networking** | **Policies** and click on the + sign on the right. This will show a form to create granular policies and associate them to a specific service instance, as shown in the following screenshot:

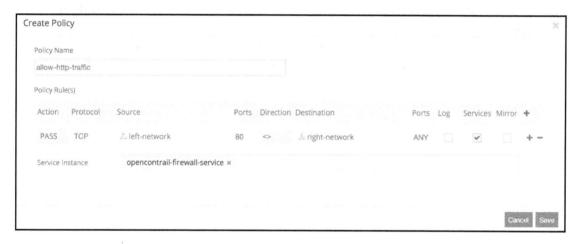

On the preceding screen, we are creating a firewall rule to allow HTTP traffic in both directions between the two virtual networks.

The preceding procedure shows how flexible and simple OpenContrail workflows allow cloud operators to create rich network topologies using virtual network functions. This is truly a powerful capability and underscores the *software* aspect of the OpenContrail SDN and NFV platform.

Summary

This chapter covered some important topics related to OpenContrail. We started off with a DevStack-based installation of OpenStack to show the integration between OpenStack and OpenContrail. We covered basic virtual network-related concepts in OpenContrail and then jumped into the flow of packets in an OpenContrail-based software-defined network. We closed the chapter with the crucial service chaining capability, which allows virtual networks to be connected to NFV entities to provide rich networking capabilities using OpenContrail. There are several more important concepts related to OpenContrail, such as more complex traffic flows, analytics, multi-level service chaining, and scalability/redundancy support. Covering all these topics will make this book unwieldy, so we recommend the reader uses this chapter as the basis for an independent study of OpenContrail.

9
Open Network Operating System (ONOS)

In Chapter 5, *Getting Started with OpenDaylight*, we showed how OpenDaylight (ODL) addresses the key needs for SDN by supporting network abstractions, rich APIs, and multi-vendor support. ODL acts as a controller for a distributed control plane, and also an on orchestrator for **Virtual Network Functions** (**VNFs**) and **Service Function Chaining** (**SFC**). Let us now focus our attention on a SDN platform called the **Open Network Operating System** (**ONOS**). While ODL primarily solves data center use cases, ONOS is architected for the carrier-grade networks requirements of performance, high availability, and scale, with well-defined abstractions.

In this chapter, we will start with an introduction to ONOS and its architecture, and we will then explore ONOS integration with Open vSwitch (OVS). We will conclude the chapter with a quick introduction to using ONOS in an OpenStack environment. We will cover the following topics in this chapter:

- Introduction to ONOS
- ONOS architecture
- Installing ONOS
- Using ONOS to manage Open vSwitch (OVS)
- ONOS and OpenStack

Introduction to ONOS

Service provider networks need agile network architectures designed to cater to exponentially-growing bandwidth demands driven by mobile devices and content distribution across the cloud. Moreover, the business imperative for creating new revenue streams offering innovative services economically requires that the network infrastructure be architected to cater to these wide-ranging requirements.

SDN provides a framework for catering to these requirements. ONOS is created with the intent of leveraging an SDN framework and enhancing it for carrier-grade service requirements providing programmable, efficient, and agile network services:

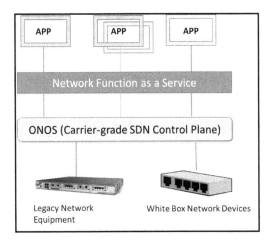

Figure 1: ONOS architecture overview

ONOS is an open source project under the **Open Networking Lab (ON.Lab)** to accelerate innovation in SDN with the objective of reducing the costs related to building and operating networks. It is developed by a partnership of service providers (AT&T, NTT Communications, Verizon), network vendors (Ciena, Cisco, Ericsson, Fujitsu, Huawei, Intel, NEC, Nokia), network operators (Internet2, CNIT, CREATE-NET), and collaborators. It is supported by the **Open Networking Foundation (ONF)**. ONOS is modeled as a complete network operating system providing features beyond the SDN controller. ONOS is an SDN network operating system (OS) for carrier-grade and mission-critical networks.

The following diagram outlines the functional progression from the **OpenFlow Controller,** focusing on providing the OpenFlow control functionality to the **SDN Controller** supporting distributed network control and to the **SDN Framework** supporting extensibility and network abstraction, and finally, to the **Network Operating System**:

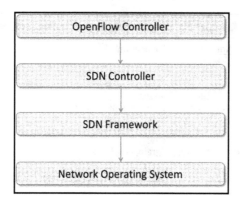

Figure 2: SDN Controller evolution

ONOS is architected to provide abstraction APIs for SDN application development, APIs to manage, monitor and program network devices. It provides virtualization, isolation, secure access, and abstraction, to networking resources managed by the network operating system. ONOS multiplexes hardware resources and software services among the SDN applications. It supports configuring network policies based on application intent and processing network events.

It is designed to operate with white box network devices to drive down the costs associated with proprietary solutions and achieve cloud-style economies of scale. ONOS has a flexible architecture that allows new networking hardware to be easily integrated into the SDN framework. Software-based orchestration reduces the OPEX costs. ONOS is implemented in Java and licensed under Apache 2.0.

Architecture of ONOS

ONOS architecture is designed specifically for carrier-grade networks' requirements of performance, high availability, and scale, with well-defined abstractions:

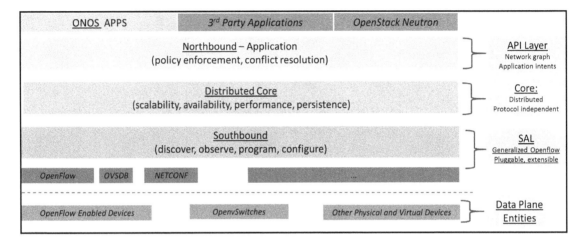

Figure 3: ONOS architecture

Let's look at the key features of ONOS, which are listed here:

- **Distributed Core**: The SDN operating system is designed to run in a cluster implementing carrier-grade network requirements for agility, resilience, fault-tolerance, high performance, elastic scalability based on application, and bandwidth demands.
- **Northbound abstraction/APIs**: These provide configuration and management services for the development of SDN applications. They support network graphs providing network view applications. Application intent frameworks enables applications to specify their network control requirements in the form of policy insulating the mechanism definition, making it easier to develop applications. They also supports device abstractions.
- **Southbound abstraction/APIs**: These provide protocol plugins to communicate with network devices. OpenFlow, OVSDB, and Netconf plugins are supported by default. A pluggable, extensible architecture enables support for protocols to communicate with legacy devices insulating the Core from the different device communication protocols.

- **Software modularity**: Modular software architecture is designed for efficient development, deployment, and maintenance. It also facilitates contributions from the ecosystem of the open source community, development of apps, and services.

Let us now continue our learning using hands-on exercises with ONOS.

Prerequisites for installing ONOS

ONOS is built using the Java programming language, hence a Java Runtime (JRE) is required to use ONOS. It is recommended to use JRE 7 or JRE 8. We recommend using a 64-bit Ubuntu-based server for trying out ONOS. You can use VirtualBox to create this server as a virtual machine. You can download the ONOS VM from `https://wiki.onosproject.org/display/ONOS/Downloads`.

Installing ONOS

ONOS is bundled as a set of core OS components and add-on applications providing the desired functionality. In this section, let's see how to install core ONOS and add application components to it. Check `https://wiki.onosproject.org/display/ONOS/Basic+ONOS+Tutorial` for details:

1. ONOS uses Apache Karaf to package, install and manage components. In order to start ONOS, start Karaf using the `karaf` command, as shown in the following screenshot:

```
ubuntu@onos:~/onos$ karaf clean
karaf: Enabling Java debug options: -Xdebug -Xnoagent -Djava.compiler=NONE
 -Xrunjdwp:transport=dt_socket,server=y,suspend=n,address=5005
Listening for transport dt_socket at address: 5005
Welcome to Open Network Operating System (ONOS)!

    ____  _   _____  _____
   / __ \/ | / / __ \/ ___/
  / / / /  |/ / / / /\__ \
 / /_/ / /|  / /_/ /___/ /
 \____/_/ |_/\____//____/


Hit '<tab>' for a list of available commands
and '[cmd] --help' for help on a specific command.
Hit '<ctrl-d>' or type 'system:shutdown' or 'logout' to shutdown ONOS.

onos> █
```

2. ONOS comes installed with basic, yet key, components. You can use the `feature:list -i` Karaf command, as shown here:

```
onos> feature:list -i
Name                    | Version          | Installed | Repository                     | Description
--------------------------------------------------------------------------------------------------------------------------------
onos-app-mobility       | 1.3.0-SNAPSHOT   | x         | onos-app-mobility-1.3.0-SNAPSHOT | Host mobility application
standard                | 3.0.3            | x         | standard-3.0.3                 | Karaf standard feature
config                  | 3.0.3            | x         | standard-3.0.3                 | Provide OSGi ConfigAdmin support
region                  | 3.0.3            | x         | standard-3.0.3                 | Provide Region Support
package                 | 3.0.3            | x         | standard-3.0.3                 | Package commands and mbeans
http                    | 3.0.3            | x         | standard-3.0.3                 | Implementation of the OSGI HTTP Service
war                     | 3.0.3            | x         | standard-3.0.3                 | Turn Karaf as a full WebContainer
kar                     | 3.0.3            | x         | standard-3.0.3                 | Provide KAR (KARaf archive) support
webconsole              | 3.0.3            | x         | standard-3.0.3                 | Base support of the Karaf WebConsole
ssh                     | 3.0.3            | x         | standard-3.0.3                 | Provide a SSHd server on Karaf
management              | 3.0.3            | x         | standard-3.0.3                 | Provide a JMX MBeanServer and a set of MBeans in K
scr                     | 3.0.3            | x         | standard-3.0.3                 | Declarative Service support
pax-jetty               | 8.1.15.v20140411 | x         | org.ops4j.pax.web-3.1.4        | Provide Jetty engine support
pax-http                | 3.1.4            | x         | org.ops4j.pax.web-3.1.4        | Implementation of the OSGI HTTP Service
pax-http-whiteboard     | 3.1.4            | x         | org.ops4j.pax.web-3.1.4        | Provide HTTP Whiteboard pattern support
pax-war                 | 3.1.4            | x         | org.ops4j.pax.web-3.1.4        | Provide support of a full WebContainer
onos-thirdparty-base    | 1.3.0-SNAPSHOT   | x         | onos-1.3.0-SNAPSHOT            | ONOS 3rd party dependencies
onos-thirdparty-web     | 1.3.0-SNAPSHOT   | x         | onos-1.3.0-SNAPSHOT            | ONOS 3rd party dependencies for web apps
onos-api                | 1.3.0-SNAPSHOT   | x         | onos-1.3.0-SNAPSHOT            | ONOS services and model API
onos-core               | 1.3.0-SNAPSHOT   | x         | onos-1.3.0-SNAPSHOT            | ONOS core components
onos-incubator          | 1.3.0-SNAPSHOT   | x         | onos-1.3.0-SNAPSHOT            | ONOS core incubator components
onos-rest               | 1.3.0-SNAPSHOT   | x         | onos-1.3.0-SNAPSHOT            | ONOS REST API components
onos-gui                | 1.3.0-SNAPSHOT   | x         | onos-1.3.0-SNAPSHOT            | ONOS GUI console components
onos-cli                | 1.3.0-SNAPSHOT   | x         | onos-1.3.0-SNAPSHOT            | ONOS admin command console components
onos-drivers            | 1.3.0-SNAPSHOT   | x         | onos-drivers-1.3.0-SNAPSHOT    | Builtin device drivers
```

This completes the basic installation of ONOS.

Installing application components

ONOS comes with default core components. Let's now add the `onos-app-fwd` application package, which provides switching functionality.

Use the `feature:install <features>` command to install the L2 switch packages as shown in the following screenshot. Once the installation is complete, you can use the `feature:list -i` command to confirm that the L2 switch packages are installed:

```
onos> feature:install onos-app-proxyarp
onos> feature:install onos-openflow
onos> feature:install onos-app-fwd
onos>
```

This completes the configuration of a minimal ONOS setup. As seen in the architecture diagram, ONOS supports many other capabilities and as an end user, you can install and use the features you require.

```
onos-drivers           | 1.3.0-SNAPSHOT   | x         | onos-drivers-1.3.0-SNAPSHOT    | Builtin device drivers
onos-app-fwd           | 1.3.0-SNAPSHOT   | x         | onos-app-fwd-1.3.0-SNAPSHOT    | Reactive forwarding application using flow subsyst
onos-openflow          | 1.3.0-SNAPSHOT   | x         | onos-openflow-1.3.0-SNAPSHOT   | OpenFlow protocol southbound providers
onos-app-proxyarp      | 1.3.0-SNAPSHOT   | x         | onos-app-proxyarp-1.3.0-SNAPSHOT | Proxy ARP/NDP application
onos>
```

Using ONOS to manage Open vSwitch

Having installed and configured ONOS with the preceding features, let's put the setup to use by managing Open vSwitch instances using ONOS. Open vSwitch, or OVS as it is popularly called, is a virtual switch that supports OpenFlow protocols:

1. In `Chapter 4`, *SDN Networking with Open vSwitch*, we introduced Mininet as a tool to simulate an Open vSwitch-based network topology. We will continue to use Mininet to discuss how ONOS can manage OVS. The first step is to create a network topology using Mininet:

```
ubuntu@onos:~/onos$  sudo mn  --topo linear,2 --mac --switch ovsk,protocols=Open
Flow13 --controller remote --arp
*** Creating network
*** Adding controller
*** Adding hosts:
h1 h2
*** Adding switches:
s1 s2
*** Adding links:
(h1, s1) (h2, s2) (s2, s1)
*** Configuring hosts
h1 h2
*** Starting controller
c0
*** Starting 2 switches
s1 s2 ...
*** Starting CLI:
mininet>
```

2. Let us check the ONOS GUI to verify the preliminary state by pointing the web browser to `http://<ONOS_Controller_IP>:8181/index.html`:

3. Simulate network traffic using a `ping` command on the Mininet shell:

```
mininet> h1 ping -c 1 h2
PING 10.0.0.2 (10.0.0.2) 56(84) bytes of data.
64 bytes from 10.0.0.2: icmp_seq=1 ttl=64 time=44.7 ms

--- 10.0.0.2 ping statistics ---
1 packets transmitted, 1 received, 0% packet loss, time 0ms
rtt min/avg/max/mdev = 44.774/44.774/44.774/0.000 ms
mininet>
```

4. Check the node, links, and device status using the ONOS CLI command as shown in the following screenshot:

```
onos> nodes
id=127.0.0.1, address=127.0.0.1:9876, state=ACTIVE, updated=26m ago *
onos> devices
id=of:0000000000000001, available=true, role=MASTER, type=SWITCH, mfr=Nicira, Inc., hw=Open vSwitch,
sw=2.3.90, serial=None, protocol=OF_13, channelId=127.0.0.1:41206
id=of:0000000000000002, available=true, role=MASTER, type=SWITCH, mfr=Nicira, Inc., hw=Open vSwitch,
sw=2.3.90, serial=None, protocol=OF_13, channelId=127.0.0.1:41207
onos> hosts
id=00:00:00:00:00:01/-1, mac=00:00:00:00:00:01, location=of:0000000000000001/1, vlan=-1, ip(s)=[]
id=00:00:00:00:00:02/-1, mac=00:00:00:00:00:02, location=of:0000000000000002/1, vlan=-1, ip(s)=[]
onos>
```

5. We will use OVS commands to verify if the OpenFlow tables have been programmed or not:

```
root@sdnhubvm:~/onos# ovs-ofctl dump-flows s1 --protocols OpenFlow13
OFPST_FLOW reply (OF1.3) (xid=0x2):
 cookie=0x1000080a0a59f, duration=33.923s, table=0, n_packets=0, n_bytes=0, send_flow_rem priority=5,arp actions=
CONTROLLER:65535
 cookie=0x100007ec4c7db, duration=33.909s, table=0, n_packets=10, n_bytes=810, send_flow_rem priority=40000,dl_ty
pe=0x8942 actions=CONTROLLER:65535
 cookie=0x1000080a0a59f, duration=33.909s, table=0, n_packets=0, n_bytes=0, send_flow_rem priority=40000,arp acti
ons=CONTROLLER:65535
 cookie=0x1000080a08f19, duration=33.909s, table=0, n_packets=2, n_bytes=196, send_flow_rem priority=5,ip actions
=CONTROLLER:65535
 cookie=0x100007ec30ce5, duration=33.909s, table=0, n_packets=10, n_bytes=810, send_flow_rem priority=40000,dl_ty
pe=0x88cc actions=CONTROLLER:65535
 cookie=0x3000080919a1d, duration=28.311s, table=0, n_packets=1, n_bytes=98, send_flow_rem priority=10,in_port=2,
dl_src=00:00:00:00:00:02,dl_dst=00:00:00:00:00:01 actions=output:1
 cookie=0x30000809faddd, duration=21.445s, table=0, n_packets=1, n_bytes=98, send_flow_rem priority=10,in_port=1,
dl_src=00:00:00:00:00:01,dl_dst=00:00:00:00:00:02 actions=output:2
root@sdnhubvm:~/onos#
```

6. We can also check the status on the ONOS GUI. It shows a summary of **Devices**, **Links** connecting them, and **Hosts** connected to the switches:

7. Check the **Devices** status including the hardware version and the OpenFlow version:

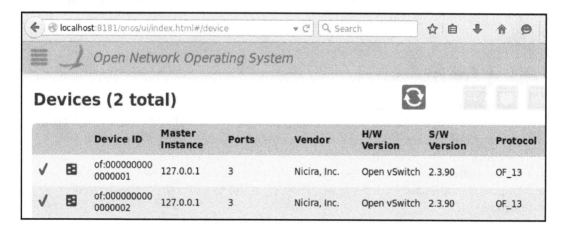

	Device ID	Master Instance	Ports	Vendor	H/W Version	S/W Version	Protocol
✓	of:0000000000000001	127.0.0.1	3	Nicira, Inc.	Open vSwitch	2.3.90	OF_13
✓	of:0000000000000002	127.0.0.1	3	Nicira, Inc.	Open vSwitch	2.3.90	OF_13

8. Check the **Hosts** status:

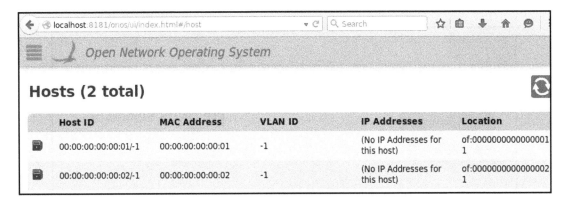

9. Disable the switching feature in ONOS to confirm that the `ping` stops, and re-enable it to verify that the `ping` resumes:

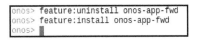

These steps show us how ONOS manages Open vSwitch and plays a role in programming the control plane and data plane of OVS.

Intent framework

Let's now install intent to communicate directly between the hosts. The ONOS intent framework allows operators to define policies using a high-level abstraction or language. It is the responsibility of the ONOS controller to translate those policies into a network configuration. This helps create networking constructs that are vendor and device-agnostic, while at the same time, it simplifies day-to-day operations. We will see that the semantics for configuration are based on intent rather than on the mechanism of the desired configuration:

1. Uninstall the switch application and add host-intent in ONOS, as shown in the following screenshot:

```
onos> feature:uninstall onos-app-fwd
onos> add-host-intent 00:00:00:00:00:01/-1 00:00:00:00:00:02/-1
Host to Host intent submitted:
HostToHostIntent{id=0xa, key=0xa, appId=DefaultApplicationId{id=2, name=org.onosproject.cli}, priority=100, r
esources=[00:00:00:00:00:01/-1, 00:00:00:00:00:02/-1], selector=DefaultTrafficSelector{criteria=[]}, treatmen
t=DefaultTrafficTreatment{immediate=[], deferred=[], transition=None, cleared=false, metadata=null}, constrai
nts=[LinkTypeConstraint{inclusive=false, types=[OPTICAL]}], one=00:00:00:00:00:01/-1, two=00:00:00:00:00:02/-
1}
onos> add-host-intent 00:00:00:00:00:02/-1 00:00:00:00:00:01/-1
Host to Host intent submitted:
HostToHostIntent{id=0xf, key=0xf, appId=DefaultApplicationId{id=2, name=org.onosproject.cli}, priority=100, r
esources=[00:00:00:00:00:02/-1, 00:00:00:00:00:01/-1], selector=DefaultTrafficSelector{criteria=[]}, treatmen
t=DefaultTrafficTreatment{immediate=[], deferred=[], transition=None, cleared=false, metadata=null}, constrai
nts=[LinkTypeConstraint{inclusive=false, types=[OPTICAL]}], one=00:00:00:00:00:02/-1, two=00:00:00:00:00:01/-
1}
```

2. Check the ONOS GUI to confirm intents are installed:

Intents (4 total)

Application ID	Key	Type	Priority	State
2 : org.onosproject.cli	0xa	HostToHostIntent	100	Installed
Resources: 00:00:00:00:00:01/-1, 00:00:00:00:00:02/-1				
Details: Constraints: [LinkTypeConstraint{inclusive=false, types=[OPTICAL]}] Host 1: 00:00:00:00:00:01/-1, Host 2: 00:00:00:00:00:02/-1				
2 : org.onosproject.cli	0xf	HostToHostIntent	100	Installed
Resources: 00:00:00:00:00:02/-1, 00:00:00:00:00:01/-1				
Details: Constraints: [LinkTypeConstraint{inclusive=false, types=[OPTICAL]}] Host 1: 00:00:00:00:00:02/-1, Host 2: 00:00:00:00:00:01/-1				
2 : org.onosproject.cli	0x0	HostToHostIntent	100	Installed
Resources: 00:00:00:00:00:01/-1, 00:00:00:00:00:02/-1				
Details: Constraints: [LinkTypeConstraint{inclusive=false, types=[OPTICAL]}] Host 1: 00:00:00:00:00:01/-1, Host 2: 00:00:00:00:00:02/-1				
2 : org.onosproject.cli	0x5	HostToHostIntent	100	Installed
Resources: 00:00:00:00:00:02/-1, 00:00:00:00:00:01/-1				
Details: Constraints: [LinkTypeConstraint{inclusive=false, types=[OPTICAL]}] Host 1: 00:00:00:00:00:02/-1, Host 2: 00:00:00:00:00:01/-1				

3. Check the OVS table to verify programming of the flow tables:

```
root@sdnhubvm:~/onos# ovs-ofctl dump-flows s1 --protocols OpenFlow13
OFPST_FLOW reply (OF1.3) (xid=0x2):
 cookie=0x100007ec4c7db, duration=2630.133s, table=0, n_packets=849, n_bytes=68769, send_flow_rem priority=40000,dl_type=0x89
42 actions=CONTROLLER:65535
 cookie=0x100007ec30ce5, duration=2630.133s, table=0, n_packets=849, n_bytes=68769, send_flow_rem priority=40000,dl_type=0x88
cc actions=CONTROLLER:65535
 cookie=0x1000080a0a59f, duration=1019.411s, table=0, n_packets=0, n_bytes=0, send_flow_rem priority=40000,arp actions=CONTRO
LLER:65535
 cookie=0x20000080919a1d, duration=622.406s, table=0, n_packets=1, n_bytes=98, send_flow_rem priority=100,in_port=2,dl_src=00
:00:00:00:00:02,dl_dst=00:00:00:00:00:01 actions=output:1
 cookie=0x200000809faddd, duration=622.405s, table=0, n_packets=1, n_bytes=98, send_flow_rem priority=100,in_port=1,dl_src=00
:00:00:00:00:01,dl_dst=00:00:00:00:00:02 actions=output:2
root@sdnhubvm:~/onos# 
```

As we can see from the preceding example, ONOS takes the intent configuration and programs the network nodes appropriately to translate the intent to the actual configuration. This abstraction enables the network administrator to focus on the required result rather than the mechanism of the desired configuration.

Distributed ONOS

Let's now see how an ONOS cluster comprising of one or more ONOS nodes, with a mechanism for syncing the network state, is a key element of the distributed ONOS core. The network switches connect with one or more ONOS nodes via the network control channel. Nodes within the same cluster communicate via the control Network. Switches in the network connect to multiple nodes to achieve resiliency and high availability:

1. Use the `onos-form-cluster` tool to create a cluster specifying a list of nodes' IP addresses.

2. Start Mininet with a set of switches, hosts, and interlinks between them:

```
distributed@mininet-vm:~/onos-byon$ ./startmn.sh
*** Creating network
*** Adding hosts:
h11 h12 h13 h14 h15 h16 h21 h22 h23 h24 h25 h26 h31 h32 h33 h34 h35 h36 h41 h42
h43 h44 h45 h46
*** Adding switches:
s1 s2 s11 s12 s13 s14
*** Adding links:
(h11, s11) (h12, s11) (h13, s11) (h14, s11) (h15, s11) (h16, s11) (h21, s12) (h2
2, s12) (h23, s12) (h24, s12) (h25, s12) (h26, s12) (h31, s13) (h32, s13) (h33,
s13) (h34, s13) (h35, s13) (h36, s13) (h41, s14) (h42, s14) (h43, s14) (h44, s14
) (h45, s14) (h46, s14) (s1, s2) (s11, s1) (s11, s2) (s12, s1) (s12, s2) (s13, s
1) (s13, s2) (s14, s1) (s14, s2)
*** Configuring hosts
h11 h12 h13 h14 h15 h16 h21 h22 h23 h24 h25 h26 h31 h32 h33 h34 h35 h36 h41 h42
h43 h44 h45 h46
*** Starting controller
c0 c1 c2
*** Starting 6 switches
s1 s2 s11 s12 s13 s14 ...
```

3. Check the ONOS status summary:

```
onos> summary
node=10.0.3.11, version=1.2.1.distributed~2016/08/08@19:35
nodes=3, devices=6, links=19, hosts=0, SCC(s)=1, flows=18, intents=0
```

4. Check the node status:

```
onos> nodes
id=10.0.3.11, address=10.0.3.11:9876, state=ACTIVE,
id=10.0.3.12, address=10.0.3.12:9876, state=ACTIVE,
id=10.0.3.13, address=10.0.3.13:9876, state=ACTIVE,
```

5. Each device has one primary master and zero or more standby controller nodes that can take over in case the primary master fails:

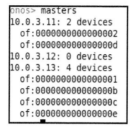

```
onos> masters
10.0.3.11: 2 devices
  of:0000000000000002
  of:000000000000000d
10.0.3.12: 0 devices
10.0.3.13: 4 devices
  of:0000000000000001
  of:000000000000000b
  of:000000000000000c
  of:000000000000000e
```

6. Check the **ONOS Summary** in the GUI:

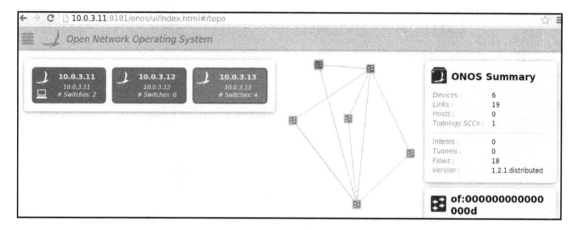

7. Rebalance the primary for optimal load distribution:

```
onos> balance-masters
onos> masters
10.0.3.11: 2 devices
  of:0000000000000002
  of:000000000000000d
10.0.3.12: 2 devices
  of:0000000000000001
  of:000000000000000e
10.0.3.13: 2 devices
  of:000000000000000b
  of:000000000000000c
```

8. Confirm OVS connects to multiple nodes:

```
root@mininet-vm:~# ovs-vsctl show
ff178c3a-58d0-4b8d-9f51-94415a5c483e
    Bridge "s14"
        Controller "tcp:10.0.3.12:6633"
            is_connected: true
        Controller "tcp:10.0.3.13:6633"
            is_connected: true
        Controller "tcp:10.0.3.11:6633"
            is_connected: true
        fail_mode: secure
        Port "s14"
            Interface "s14"
                type: internal
        Port "s14-eth1"
```

Central Office Re-architected as Datacenter

Central Office Re-architected as Datacenter (**CORD**), available at `http://opencord.org/`, is a collaborative effort of AT&T and Open Networking Lab to model Telco Central Office as a data center for rapid service creation and monetization. It aims to leverage SDN and NFV innovations from the data center and commodity hardware to build agile, cost-effective networks deriving significant CAPEX and OPEX savings over an existing, disparate range of proprietary network devices.

CORD re-architects the Central Office as a data center by unifying SDN, NFV, and cloud technologies. The SDN approach of separating data and control planes with standard APIs enables the leveraging of commodity hardware based on merchant silicon driving down costs and making control planes programmable in supporting innovation. NFV makes the move to virtual machines from hardware appliances and cloud support scalable. Resilient network topologies thereby deriving cost savings and platform for innovation:

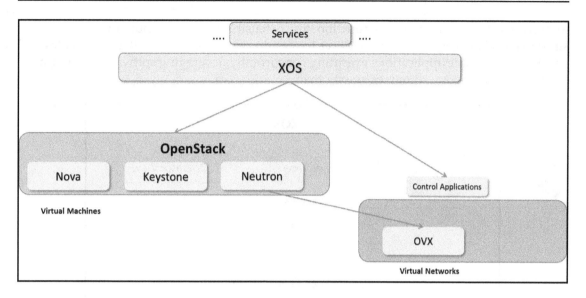

Figure 4: CORD architecture

OpenStack, **ONOS**, and **XOS** form the software building blocks for the CORD architecture.

OpenStack provides core IaaS, supporting the provisioning of **Virtual Machines** and **Virtual Networks**.

ONOS serves as a platform for implementing the control applications. **OpenVirteX (OVX)**, is an ONOS sub-system invoked via OpenStack's Neutron API and is responsible for embedding virtual networks in the underlying switching fabric. You can explore more about OVX at `http://ovx.onlab.us/getting-started/tutorial/`.

Extensible Cloud Operating System

The **Extensible Cloud Operating System (XOS)**, available at `http://xosproject.org/`, implements the creation and management of services as a core operation. XOS treats everything as a service and provides a framework for implementing multi-tenant services. XOS is modeled as an *anything-as-a-service operating system*, providing general programming abstractions for network-wide operations.

XOS is architected as a set of core functionality, extensible by services built over it. It supports mechanisms to combine services to create a new functionality. It also provides support for multiple applications executing concurrently, leveraging software services, and multiplexing hardware resources among them:

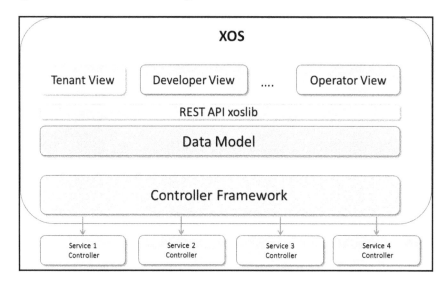

Figure 4: XOS architecture

XOS provides a **Service Controller** interface that is logically centralized. It provides multi-tenancy support and the ability to scale elastically across a set of service instances. A logically centralized controller with distributed service instances is a core design aspect of XOS, which is central to supporting the carrier-grade requirements of scale and resiliency. The **Controller Framework** provides distributed state management. The **Data Model** records the logically centralized state of the XOS system. It binds the services and provides a mechanism for them to interoperate efficiently. **Xoslib** provides the RESTful HTTP interface for the operations supported by the **Data Model** objects.

Users interact with XOS with a set of views, depending on the objective.

XOS is a service orchestration layer that unifies the management of OpenStack-provided infrastructure services and ONOS-provided control-plane services.

Summary

This chapter provided an introduction to ONOS. After covering the ONOS architecture in brief, we showed how ONOS can manage Open vSwitch. With OVS being the most-used virtual switch in OpenStack deployment, this step was important to understand the relationship between ONOS and OpenStack. We touched upon growing an application for the SDN framework on the service provider network. We also described how to install and configure an ONOS system and outlined the landscape where ONOS fits in the context of OpenStack and XOS. Finally, we summarized the role of XOS as a service orchestration layer unifying OpenStack management.

10
OVN and Open vSwitch Enhancements

In Chapter 3, *SDN Protocols*, we introduced Open vSwitch (OVS) the most popular virtual switch in OpenStack deployment and in Chapter 4, *SDN Networking with Open vSwitch*, we peeked under the hood to gain insights on the building blocks of OpenFlow based networking with Open vSwitch, discussing how it communicates with SDN controllers and interfaces with OpenStack Neutron. This chapter aims to build on this to gain understanding on Open vSwitch packet flows in OpenStack Neutron. It will start with introducing various interfaces, such as br-int, br-tun, and br-ex, and explain how Neutron uses these OVS switches to offer networking as a service.

SDN at layer 2 and 3 along with **Network Function Virtualization** (NFV) features at layers 4 and above, executing in general purpose servers with Linux OS, are emerging as an attractive alternative to propriety solutions from networking vendors. Open vSwitch continues to evolve to address performance requirements of use cases such as NFV and high performance switching.

In this chapter, we will outline the limitations in the classic Neutron architecture and move on to talk about solutions such as the **Distributed Virtual Router** (DVR) and the **Open Virtual Network** (OVN), an extension to Open vSwitch and Neutron Dragonflow.

We will cover the following topics in this chapter:

- Open vSwitch components in network node
- Neutron Distributed Virtual Router (DVR)
- Open vSwitch components in compute node
- Open virtual network OVN
- Dragonflow
- OVS-DPKD

Open vSwitch components in network node

Let us begin with an overview of Open vSwitch bridges created in the network node.

The Open vSwitch agent creates the following OVS bridge interfaces as per configuration options:

- `br-int`: Network service components connect to this OVS Integration Bridge to offer services such as DHCP, SNAT, and routing. Compute instances connect to this bridge to obtain network services.
- `br-vlan`, `br-tun`: This communicates with compute nodes on the Tunnel Bridge. It has open flow rules to match and forward the traffic destined to the services on the network node or else drops the packets.

- `br-ex`: Traffic to external network flows through `br-ex` via the interface in the router name space, which connects to the `br-ex` as tap interface.

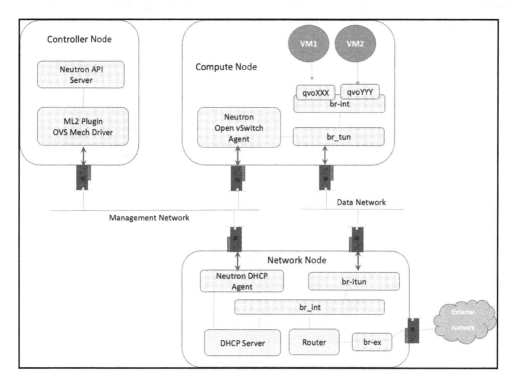

Figure 1: OVS bridges on a network node

Neutron DHCP

The DHCP agent managing the `qdhcp` network namespaces provides DHCP services for instances.

Neutron routing

The Neutron router routes traffic between north-south and east-west network traffic and performs DNAT/SNAT via a network namespace with a set of routing tables and iptables rules. It also routes metadata traffic between instances and the metadata agent.

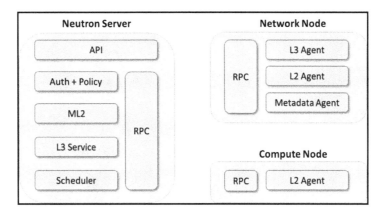

Figure 2: Router service on a Network Node

`neutron-l3-agent` implementation leverages Linux IP stacks and iptables to provide L3, and NAT services to compute instances connected via Neutron L2 networks. The L3-agent supports multiple routers uses network namespaces to provide isolated forwarding contexts.

Neutron DVR

The network node is single point of failure in the classic Neutron virtual routing architecture presented previously. All traffic gets directed to the network node to be routed resulting in performance bottleneck and scalability limitations.

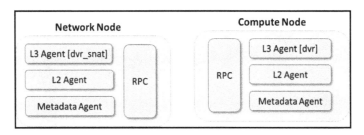

Figure 4: Neutron DVR

The Neutron DVR solves the performance and scale problem by distributing east/west L3 forwarding and north/south DNAT to the compute nodes. The `neutron-13-agent` in the compute node supports the routing between tenant and external networks for instances with a floating IP address.

The network node continues to support routing between tenant and external networks for instances with a fixed IP address and SNAT services for north-south network traffic.

Open vSwitch components in compute host

The Open vSwitch agent manages connectivity among virtual switches and supports interaction via virtual ports with other network components such as namespaces to provide network isolation, and Linux Bridges to support security groups. Integration Bridge in compute node supports interfaces to virtual machines. The Open vSwitch agent creates the following OVS bridge interfaces as per configuration options.

The Integration Bridge is usually named `br-int` and each instance is plugged into the it via a **veth** port. This carries traffic to and from the instance (VM) via a **Linux Bridge**.

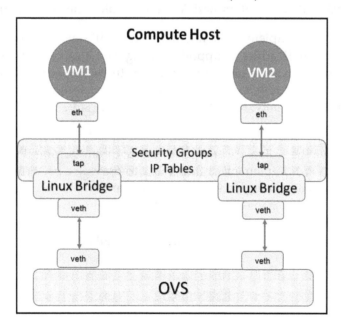

Figure 3: OVS on a compute node

Open vSwitch (**OVS**) cannot connect with iptables to implement security groups. Linux Bridge is used between each instance (**VM**) and the OVS Integration Bridge `br-int` to implements security groups. Linux Bridge the traffic between the **veth** peer port and **tap** interface which connects to the instance.

The `br-int` adds a VLAN ID tag to the packet header for the untagged packets received from the instance based on the network-id and strips off the VLAN ID for the packets to the instance. Each network is assigned a unique VLAN ID and is classified based on the tag.

The `br-tun` connects the Integration Bridge `br-int` via a patch interface. Tunnel Bridge (`br-tun`) translates VLAN-tagged traffic from the Integration Bridge (`br-int`) into tunnel IDs depending on the tunnel type (VXLAN, GRE).

OVN – Native Virtual Networking Open vSwitch

Open vSwitch Virtual Networking (**OVN**) augments Open vSwitch by adding SDN constructs of logical switches, routers, and ACLs to simplify the OVS Neutron integration.

The `neutron-l3-agent` implementation with the Linux IP stack and iptables to provide L3 services and overlapping IP address support by using the Linux network namespace has performance bottlenecks in some deployment architectures. The addition of the Linux Bridge between instances and the `br-int` bridge to support security groups using iptables introduces performance penalty. Refer to `http://openvswitch.org/support/slides/OVN-Vancouver.pdf` for details.

OVN aims to improve the scalability and performance by supporting IPv4 and IPv6 natively in the OVS. OVN implements a flow cache to provide a performance boost. OVN implements firewalls natively as flows in OVS using the Kernel `conntrack` module directly from OVS. Communication is via database updates to the `ovsdb` database, reducing the overhead associated with `rabbitmq` RPC. Refer to `http://openvswitch.org/support/dist-docs/ovn-architecture.7.html` for architectural details.

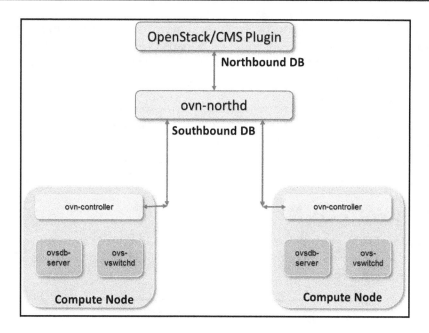

Figure 5: OVN components

Neutron's OVN plugin communicates via OVSDB to configure OVN's northbound database through the `ovn-northd` interface. The Neutron OVN ML2 driver translates configuration requests for resources into OVN's data model. OVN creates resources by updating the associated tables in the OVN northbound database.

The `ovn-northd` translates logical network configuration from the OVN northbound database into logical data path flows in the OVN southbound DB. The `ovn-controller` daemon running in each host receives the logical state information and converts it into OpenFlow flows that reflect the local physical view.

Drivers for OVN

The primary objective of OVN is to simplify the OpenStack Neutron architecture by subsuming core networking functionalities that are best implemented using Open vSwitch.

OpenStack Neutron not only provides database APIs but also defines the networking entities such as networks, ports, subnets, routers, and so on. The implementation for these entities is left to plugins and drivers. In terms of network isolation, VXLAN, VLAN, and GRE are the primary network types. These network types are implemented using OVS or Linux Bridge on the virtual network. Neutron supports security groups in order to secure network traffic but it is a standalone entity within Neutron.

Neutron also is designed to be agnostic to physical networks. However, in real world deployment it is common to connect virtual workloads (VM instances) on virtual networks to legacy devices that are connected only to physical networks. Neutron does not provide a native support for this bridging.

OVN aims to provide a more native networking abstraction that unifies different network types and their implementation using Open vSwitch. It also brings in networking services such as DHCP and security/ACLs into its fold, thereby providing a more complete and integrated L2 and L3 networking solution for OpenStack.

Working with OVN

Let's now explore OVN, starting with building and installing OVN from source code. You can checkout the stable version of the source code from GitHub. OVS version 2.5 is stable at the time of writing this book.

```
$ git clone -b branch-2.5 https://github.com/openvswitch/ovs.git
~/OVS# ./boot.sh
~/OVS# ./configure
~/OVS# make
```

The `ovs-sandbox` component in the Open vSwitch codebase presents an OVS-based software simulated network environment, which is a great choice for hands-on Open vSwitch tutorials. Running `ovs-sandbox` with the `--ovn` flag sets up the Open vSwitch environment for OVN, which includes creating the `OVN_Northbound` and `OVN_Southbound` databases, executing `ovn` daemons, and building `ovn` utilities such as `ovn-nbctl` and `ovn-sbctl`.

Refer to `https://github.com/openvswitch/ovs/tree/master/tutorial/ovn`.

Let us proceed with the series of steps to explore the working of OVN:

1. Creates a dummy Open vSwitch environment.

```
~/ovs# make sandbox SANDBOXFLAGS="--ovn"
```

2. Configure a logical switch.

```
ovn-nbctl lswitch-add sw0
```

3. Add ports to the logical switch.

```
ovn-nbctl lport-add sw0 sw0-port1
ovn-nbctl lport-add sw0 sw0-port2
```

4. Configure a MAC address.

```
ovn-nbctl lport-set-addresses sw0-port1 00:00:00:00:00:01
ovn-nbctl lport-set-addresses sw0-port2 00:00:00:00:00:02
```

5. Check the OVN_Northbound database.

```
root@controller:~# ovn-nbctl show
    lswitch 73fd307e-f50f-49f9-8733-e939e46c484a (sw0)
        lport sw0-port2
            addresses: ["00:00:00:00:00:02"]
        lport sw0-port1
            addresses: ["00:00:00:00:00:01"]
    lswitch 3e32584a-6ec1-43ea-a456-8951bafdacd2 (sw0)
```

6. Check the database OVN_Southbound.

```
root@controller:~# ovn-sbctl show
Chassis "56b18105-5706-46ef-80c4-ff20979ab068"
    Encap geneve
        ip: "127.0.0.1"
```

7. Add a logical port to the local OVS bridge, br-int.

```
ovs-vsctl add-port br-int lport1 -- set Interface lport1 external_ids:iface-id=sw0-port1
ovs-vsctl add-port br-int lport2 -- set Interface lport2 external_ids:iface-id=sw0-port2
```

8. Check contents of the OVS bridge.

```
root@controller:~# ovs-vsctl show
8f3a0886-5794-4399-9065-3124147040c6
    Bridge br-int
        fail_mode: secure
        Port br-int
            Interface br-int
                type: internal
        Port "lport2"
            Interface "lport2"
        Port "lport1"
            Interface "lport1"
```

The `ovn-controller` monitors the updates to local switch configuration matching OVN logical ports. Upon an `iface-id` match, the `ovn-controller` will associate the local ports with OVN logical ports.

9. Check the port bindings in the `OVN_Southbound` database.

```
root@controller:~# ovn-sbctl show
Chassis "56b18105-5706-46ef-80c4-ff20979ab068"
    Encap geneve
        ip: "127.0.0.1"
    Port_Binding "sw0-port1"
    Port_Binding "sw0-port2"

    # ovsdb-client dump OVN_Southbound
```

actions	external_ids	match	pipeline	priority	table_id
"drop;"	{stage-name=ls_in_port_sec}	"eth.src[40]"	ingress	100	0
"drop;"	{stage-name=ls_in_port_sec}	vlan.present	ingress	100	0
"next;"	{stage-name=ls_in_port_sec}	"inport == \"sw0-port1\" && eth.src == {00:00:00:00:00:01}"	ingress	50	0
"next;"	{stage-name=ls_in_port_sec}	"inport == \"sw0-port2\" && eth.src == {00:00:00:00:00:02}"	ingress	50	0
"next;"	{stage-name=ls_out_pre_acl}	"1"	egress	0	0
"next;"	{stage-name=ls_in_pre_acl}	"1"	ingress	0	1
"next;"	{stage-name=ls_out_acl}	"1"	egress	0	1
"output;"	{stage-name=ls_out_port_sec}	eth.mcast	egress	100	2
"output;"	{stage-name=ls_out_port_sec}	"outport == \"sw0-port1\" && eth.dst == {00:00:00:00:00:01}"	egress	50	2
"output;"	{stage-name=ls_out_port_sec}	"outport == \"sw0-port2\" && eth.dst == {00:00:00:00:00:02}"	egress	50	2
"next;"	{stage-name=ls_in_acl}	"1"	ingress	0	2
"outport = \"_MC_flood\"; output;"	{stage-name="ls_in_l2_lkup"}	eth.mcast	ingress	100	3
"outport = \"sw0-port1\"; output;"	{stage-name="ls_in_l2_lkup"}	"eth.dst == 00:00:00:00:00:01"	ingress	50	3
"outport = \"sw0-port2\"; output;"	{stage-name="ls_in_l2_lkup"}	"eth.dst == 00:00:00:00:00:02"	ingress	50	3

The preceding logical flow table depicts contents of `OVN_Southbound` edited to capture important elements.

The `ovn-controller` translates the logical flows into OpenFlow flows in the local host.

Now let's check the OVS OpenFlow table contents of `br-int` edited to depict elements important for this discussion. Notice the similarity in the table contents as logical flow data is programmed into OpenFlow flows.

```
# ovs-ofctl  dump-flows br-int
```

table_id	priority	Actions
table=0	priority=100	in_port=1 actions=resubmit(16)
table=0	priority=100	in_port=2 actions=resubmit(16)
table=16	priority=100	vlan_tci=0x1000/0x1000 actions=drop
table=16	priority=100	dl_src=01:00:00:00:00:00/01:00:00:00:00:00 actions=drop
table=16	priority=50	dl_src=00:00:00:00:00:01 actions=resubmit(17)
table=16	priority=50	dl_src=00:00:00:00:00:02 actions=resubmit(17)
table=17	priority=0	actions=resubmit(18)
table=18	priority=0	actions=resubmit(19)
table=19	priority=100	dl_dst=01:00:00:00:00:00/01:00:00:00:00:00 actions=resubmit(32)
table=19	priority=50	dl_dst=00:00:00:00:00:01 actions=resubmit(32)
table=19	priority=50	dl_dst=00:00:00:00:00:02 actions=resubmit(32)
table=49	priority=0	actions=resubmit(50)
table=50	priority=100	dl_dst=01:00:00:00:00:00/01:00:00:00:00:00 actions=resubmit(64)
table=50	priority=50	dl_dst=00:00:00:00:00:01 actions=resubmit(64)
table=50	priority=50	dl_dst=00:00:00:00:00:02 actions=resubmit(64)
table=64	priority=100	actions=output:1
table=64	priority=100	actions=output:2

OVN firewall

Let's now see how OVN implements the firewall natively as flows in OVS:

1. Configure ACL rules to allow ICMP packets and SSH connections and drop all other IP traffic.

```
root@controller:~# ovn-nbctl acl-add sw0 from-lport 1002 "inport == \"sw0-port1\
" && ip" allow-related
root@controller:~# ovn-nbctl acl-add sw0 to-lport 1002 "outport == \"sw0-port1\"
 && ip && icmp" allow-related
root@controller:~# ovn-nbctl acl-add sw0 to-lport 1002 "outport == \"sw0-port1\"
 && ip && tcp && tcp.dst == 22" allow-related
root@controller:~# ovn-nbctl acl-add sw0 to-lport 1001 "outport == \"sw0-port1\"
 && ip" drop
```

2. Check the ACL updates to the OVN_Northbound database:

```
root@controller:~#  ovn-nbctl acl-list sw0
from-lport  1002 (inport == "sw0-port1" && ip) allow-related
  to-lport  1002 (outport == "sw0-port1" && ip && icmp) allow-related
  to-lport  1002 (outport == "sw0-port1" && ip && tcp && tcp.dst == 22) allow-related
  to-lport  1001 (outport == "sw0-port1" && ip) drop
```

3. Check the ACL updates to the OVN_Southbound database:

```
~# ovn-sbctl lflow-list
```

Pipeline: ingress

table=0(ls_in_port_sec)	priority= 100	match=(eth.src[40])	action=(drop;)
table=0(ls_in_port_sec)	priority= 100	match=(vlan.present)	action=(drop;)
table=0(ls_in_port_sec)	priority= 50	match=(inport == "sw0-port1" && eth.src == {00:00:00:00:00:01})	action=(next;)
table=0(ls_in_port_sec)	priority= 50	match=(inport == "sw0-port2" && eth.src == {00:00:00:00:00:02})	action=(next;)
table=1(ls_in_pre_acl)	priority= 100	match=(ip)	action=(ct_next;)
table=1(ls_in_pre_acl)	priority= 0	match=(1)	action=(next;)
table=2(ls_in_acl)	priority=65535	match=(!ct.est && ct.rel && !ct.new && !ct.inv)	action=(next;)
table=2(ls_in_acl)	priority=65535	match=(ct.est && !ct.rel && !ct.new && !ct.inv)	action=(next;)
table=2(ls_in_acl)	priority=65535	match=(ct.inv)	action=(drop;)
table=2(ls_in_acl)	priority= 2002	match=(ct.new && (inport == "sw0-port1" && ip))	action=(ct_commit; next;)
table=2(ls_in_acl)	priority= 1	match=(ip)	action=(ct_commit; next;)
table=2(ls_in_acl)	priority= 0	match=(1)	action=(next;)
table=3(ls_in_l2_lkup)	priority= 100	match=(eth.mcast)	action=(outport = "_MC_flood"; output;)
table=3(ls_in_l2_lkup)	priority= 50	match=(eth.dst == 00:00:00:00:00:01)	action=(outport = "sw0-port1"; output;)
table=3(ls_in_l2_lkup)	priority= 50	match=(eth.dst == 00:00:00:00:00:02)	action=(outport = "sw0-port2"; output;)

The table depicts contents of logical flow, showing the contents of the `ls_in_pre_acl` and `ls_in_acl`, ACL stages. In table 1, `ls_in_pre_acl` maches the IP traffic and with the action `ct_next` passes it through the connection tracker. `ls_in_acl` (table 2) applies policies on the connection state fields.

Pipeline: egress

table=0(ls_out_pre_acl)	priority= 100	match=(ip)	action=(ct_next;)
table=0(ls_out_pre_acl)	priority= 0	match=(1)	action=(next;)
table=1(ls_out_acl)	priority=65535	match=(!ct.est && ct.rel && !ct.new && !ct.inv)	action=(next;)
table=1(ls_out_acl)	priority=65535	match=(ct.est && !ct.rel && !ct.new && !ct.inv)	action=(next;)
table=1(ls_out_acl)	priority=65535	match=(ct.inv)	action=(drop;)
table=1(ls_out_acl)	priority= 2002	match=(ct.new && (outport == "sw0-port1" && ip && icmp))	action=(ct_commit; next;)
table=1(ls_out_acl)	priority= 2002	match=(ct.new && (outport == "sw0-port1" && ip && tcp && tcp.dst == 22))	action=(ct_commit; next;)
table=1(ls_out_acl)	priority= 2001	match=(outport == "sw0-port1" && ip)	action=(drop;)
table=1(ls_out_acl)	priority= 1	match=(ip)	action=(ct_commit; next;)
table=1(ls_out_acl)	priority= 0	match=(1)	action=(next;)
table=2(ls_out_port_sec)	priority= 100	match=(eth.mcast)	action=(output;)
table=2(ls_out_port_sec)	priority= 50	match=(outport == "sw0-port1" && eth.dst == {00:00:00:00:00:01})	action=(output;)
table=2(ls_out_port_sec)	priority= 50	match=(outport == "sw0-port2" && eth.dst == {00:00:00:00:00:02})	action=(output;)

Table depicts contents of logical flow edited to show the contents of the ACL stages `ls_out_pre_acl`, and `ls_out_acl`. In Table 0, `ls_out_pre_acl` matches IP traffic and passes it through the connection tracker which applies policies on the connection state fields.

OVN and OpenStack

Let us now turn our attention to the integration of OVN with OpenStack. The main element of this integration is the mapping of OpenStack Neutron objects to that of OVN. We will use DevStack to demonstrate different OpenStack operations and then show the corresponding OVN entities.

Running OVN using DevStack

We will now show you how to install and use OVN using DevStack. OVN has been extensively tested on Ubuntu 14.04 so we recommend that as the version to try with these steps:

1. The first step is to check out DevStack and OVN from GitHub.

```
openstack@openstack:~$ git clone http://git.openstack.org/openstack-dev/devstack.git
Cloning into 'devstack'...
remote: Counting objects: 35631, done.
remote: Compressing objects: 100% (16978/16978), done.
remote: Total 35631 (delta 25321), reused 28070 (delta 18163)
Receiving objects: 100% (35631/35631), 7.22 MiB | 959.00 KiB/s, done.
Resolving deltas: 100% (25321/25321), done.
Checking connectivity... done.
openstack@openstack:~$ git clone http://git.openstack.org/openstack/networking-ovn.git
Cloning into 'networking-ovn'...
remote: Counting objects: 5449, done.
remote: Compressing objects: 100% (2926/2926), done.
remote: Total 5449 (delta 3726), reused 3909 (delta 2358)
Receiving objects: 100% (5449/5449), 1.50 MiB | 487.00 KiB/s, done.
Resolving deltas: 100% (3726/3726), done.
Checking connectivity... done.
openstack@openstack:~$
```

2. Copy the sample `local.conf` from OVN to DevStack. If you view the `local.conf` file you will notice that the Neutron L2 agent (`q-agt`) is disabled. This is because OVN does not rely on the Neutron L2 Agent. It directly programs Open vSwitch using OpenFlow and OVSDB.

```
openstack@openstack:~$ cd devstack/
openstack@openstack:~/devstack$ cp ../networking-ovn/devstack/local.conf.sample local.conf
```

3. Run the `stack.sh` command from DevStack to set up your DevStack environment.

```
./stack.sh
```

4. Once DevStack runs successfully, we will open the contents of the Neutron ML2 configuration file to see that OVN is the ML2 driver. Note that OVN uses Geneve as the default tunneling/encapsulation technology to provide network segmentation. The ML2 configuration file is located at `/etc/neutron/plugins/ml2/ml2_conf.ini`. The relevant snippet related to OVN ML2 configuration is shown here.

```
[ml2]
tenant_network_types = geneve
extension_drivers = port_security
type_drivers = local,flat,vlan,geneve
mechanism_drivers = ovn,logger
```

This completes the setup of OVN with OpenStack using DevStack. We will now focus on the mapping of Neutron objects to that of OVN.

Mapping of Neutron and OVN object models

As mentioned earlier, the OVN Northbound API receive, incoming requests from the OVN Neutron ML2 driver and translates the Neutron data model to the OVN data model. We will now see the objects in the OVN data model and how they are mapped to Neutron objects.

In a DevStack environment a few Neutron networks and a router is created automatically as part of DevStack setup, as seen from the output of `neutron net-list` and `neutron router-list` commands.

```
openstack@openstack:~/devstack$ neutron net-list
+--------------------------------------+---------+----------------------------------------------------+
| id                                   | name    | subnets                                            |
+--------------------------------------+---------+----------------------------------------------------+
| 2dc3b29e-fc19-4aae-b9d0-d3b9f6cd74d6 | public  | c53edac3-0318-4adc-9bb9-678fdb649405               |
|                                      |         | 16f1893c-9f53-4b31-8d90-ce92fcbfedf7               |
| 553c8607-2678-46df-b4e7-635239140647 | private | d5721586-856b-4f79-87f5-e229ea46950e 2001:db8:8000::/64 |
|                                      |         | 34e96a6d-8748-4cda-b545-ece9c2842105 10.0.0.0/24   |
+--------------------------------------+---------+----------------------------------------------------+

openstack@openstack:~/devstack$ neutron router-list
+--------------------------------------+---------+----------------------------------------------------+
| id                                   | name    | external_gateway_info                              |
+--------------------------------------+---------+----------------------------------------------------+
| 1720613f-8490-46fe-a67e-f797f8eb0d0f | router1 | {"network_id": "2dc3b29e-fc19-4aae-b9d0-d3b9f6cd74d6", "external_fixed_ips": |
|                                      |         | [{"subnet_id": "16f1893c-9f53-4b31-8d90-ce92fcbfedf7", "ip_address": |
|                                      |         | "172.24.4.9"}, {"subnet_id": "c53edac3-0318-4adc-9bb9-678fdb649405", |
|                                      |         | "ip_address": "2001:db8::1"}]}                     |
+--------------------------------------+---------+----------------------------------------------------+
```

In order to view the OVN object, we will start with a simple `ovn-nbctl show` command that shows the summary of the entire OVN data model.

```
openstack@openstack:~/devstack$ ovn-nbctl show
    switch bc27e3a8-056f-44eb-90fb-468f7d9f7d45 (neutron-553c8607-2678-46df-b4e7-635239140647)
        port e1f670c1-a7d8-402a-90ef-1aa0a0a26ea2
            addresses: ["fa:16:3e:79:23:76 2001:db8:8000::1"]
        port ca37cce2-9d01-4289-acc0-7892af566695
            addresses: ["fa:16:3e:c3:83:b9 10.0.0.1"]
    switch 80abca15-01f8-4367-820c-062c55ddbd7d (neutron-2dc3b29e-fc19-4aae-b9d0-d3b9f6cd74d6)
        port provnet-2dc3b29e-fc19-4aae-b9d0-d3b9f6cd74d6
            addresses: ["unknown"]
        port 1c16f49d-1bb2-463f-a32a-b3506bf44eb9
            addresses: ["fa:16:3e:9d:ce:3d 172.24.4.9 2001:db8::1"]
    router a99119fb-4756-4f2c-baa9-e9ca96bbee8b (neutron-1720613f-8490-46fe-a67e-f797f8eb0d0f)
        port lrp-ca37cce2-9d01-4289-acc0-7892af566695
            mac: "fa:16:3e:c3:83:b9"
            networks: ["10.0.0.1/24"]
        port lrp-e1f670c1-a7d8-402a-90ef-1aa0a0a26ea2
            mac: "fa:16:3e:79:23:76"
            networks: ["2001:db8:8000::1/64"]
openstack@openstack:~/devstack$
```

As you can see, similar to the Neutron command output, the OVN show command displays two switches (networks) and one router.

Network and logical switch

The Neutron network object is mapped to a logical switch object in OVN. The idea of a logical switch is to provide a unified layer 2 domain for VM instances, containers, and even legacy/physical devices.

To demonstrate this mapping, we will first create a network in Neutron using the CLI command.

```
openstack@openstack:~/devstack$ neutron net-create OVN-Test-Network
```

Next, we will execute the OVN command for listing logical switches.

```
openstack@openstack:~/devstack$ ovn-nbctl ls-list
80abca15-01f8-4367-820c-062c55ddbd7d (neutron-2dc3b29e-fc19-4aae-b9d0-d3b9f6cd74d6)
bc27e3a8-056f-44eb-90fb-468f7d9f7d45 (neutron-553c8607-2678-46df-b4e7-635239140647)
18fffb03-03e3-4797-8f7f-4601b6b4ff04 (neutron-b0f42bd3-3807-4a3d-a6e4-667ab9379ad7)
```

The `ovn-nbctl ls-list` displays all the logical switches in the OVN controller. The output shows two parameters in each row. The first one is the UUID assigned to the logical switch within OVN. The text in parentheses is the name of the logical switch. The name is derived by concatenating `neutron-` to the UUID of the Neutron network.

Subnet and DHCP

The Neutron subnet object is mapped to DHCP options in OVN. You can create a subnet using Neutron CLI and then using the `ovn-nbctl` command, as shown in the following example, to view the mapping.

```
openstack@openstack:~/devstack$ neutron subnet-create --name OVN-Test-Subnet OVN-Test-Network 20.20.20.0/24


openstack@openstack:~/devstack$ ovn-nbctl dhcp-options-list
ba0b3a7d-8290-4a80-b6eb-c81d12c6f24f
e77c90d0-dac4-410f-a052-9202ef25ddac
777592cb-5a27-4d79-9393-8dfd866f9bbf
openstack@openstack:~/devstack$ ovn-nbctl dhcp-options-get-options e77c90d0-dac4-410f-a052-9202ef25ddac
server_mac=fa:16:3e:7c:6c:82
router=20.20.20.1
server_id=20.20.20.1
mtu=1442
lease_time=43200
openstack@openstack:~/devstack$
```

The `ovn-nbctl dhcp-options-list` shows all the subnet mappings. You can use the `dhcp-options-get-options` sub-command to view the details of a specific subnet mapping.

Neutron port and OVN port

The `port` object in Neutron is mapped to either a switch port or a router port in OVN. In Neutron you can use the `device_owner` attribute to distinguish between a network port versus a router port. In OVN they are two different port objects. This distinction is useful from a management perspective.

We will create a Neutron port and then show the OVN commands to view the corresponding OVN object.

```
openstack@openstack:~/devstack$ neutron port-create OVN-Test-Network
```

If we execute the `ovn-nbctl show` command, we can see that a logical switch and a switch port corresponding to the Neutron network and port are displayed. We can see that the `port` has been assigned an IP address of `20.20.20.7`.

```
openstack@openstack:~/devstack$ ovn-nbctl show
    switch bc27e3a8-056f-44eb-90fb-468f7d9f7d45 (neutron-553c8607-2678-46df-b4e7-635239140647)
        port e1f670c1-a7d8-402a-90ef-1aa0a0a26ea2
            addresses: ["fa:16:3e:79:23:76 2001:db8:8000::1"]
        port ca37cce2-9d01-4289-acc0-7892af566695
            addresses: ["fa:16:3e:c3:83:b9 10.0.0.1"]
    switch 80abca15-01f8-4367-820c-062c55ddbd7d (neutron-2dc3b29e-fc19-4aae-b9d0-d3b9f6cd74d6)
        port provnet-2dc3b29e-fc19-4aae-b9d0-d3b9f6cd74d6
            addresses: ["unknown"]
        port 1c16f49d-1bb2-463f-a32a-b3506bf44eb9
            addresses: ["fa:16:3e:9d:ce:3d 172.24.4.9 2001:db8::1"]
    switch 18fffb03-03e3-4797-8f7f-4601b6b4ff04 (neutron-b0f42bd3-3807-4a3d-a6e4-667ab9379ad7)
        port 4c2072c4-a984-4a83-87c0-73e0eea13918
            addresses: ["fa:16:3e:18:f4:84 20.20.20.7"]
    router a99119fb-4756-4f2c-baa9-e9ca96bbee8b (neutron-1720613f-8490-46fe-a67e-f797f8eb0d0f)
        port lrp-ca37cce2-9d01-4289-acc0-7892af566695
            mac: "fa:16:3e:c3:83:b9"
            networks: ["10.0.0.1/24"]
        port lrp-e1f670c1-a7d8-402a-90ef-1aa0a0a26ea2
            mac: "fa:16:3e:79:23:76"
            networks: ["2001:db8:8000::1/64"]
```

The highlighted section also shows the MAC address of the port. You can explore the `ovn-nbctl lsp-list` and related commands to view OVN port information.

Other mappings

We have looked at the three important Neutron objects and their OVN mappings. The other important entities are routers and security groups.

The Neutron router is mapped to a logical router in OVN. This is a simple and direct mapping. You can use `ovn-nbctl lr-list` and related commands for the OVN logical router.

The security group is the next most important entity. In Neutron, users can create security groups and the corresponding rules independently and then apply them to VM at the time of instantiation. The corresponding port stores the security group reference.

In OVN security groups are mapped to an **Access Control List** (**ACL**) object and it has a direct relationship with the port as well as the logical switch. This makes it a more cohesive mapping when compared to Neutron.

OVN's roadmap for OpenStack

OVN aims to be the next level replacement for the OVS plugin in OpenStack Neutron. By providing much more logical network constructs around Open vSwitch, OVN is simplifying the integration for the most widely deployed virtual switch. The project is most easily tested in a DevStack environment but full Linux packages are available already. We hope the introduction provided here will help readers explore this highly anticipated networking project within OpenStack.

Neutron Dragonflow

Dragonflow is a distributed SDN controller implementation for OpenStack Neutron. Neutron Dragonflow adopts a distributed approach to mitigate the scaling issues outlined in the reference Neutron implementation for certain deployment scenarios. Similar to DVR, the load is distributed to the compute node executing local controller. However, unlike DVR, Dragonflow follows agentless design and SDN principles to implement Neutron APIs.

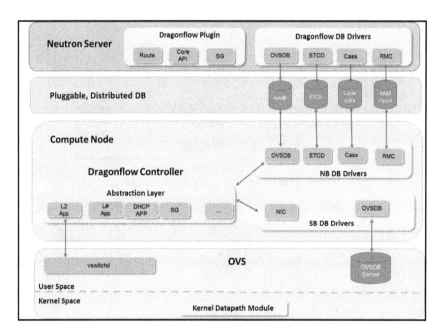

Figure 6: Neutron Dragonflow components

DragonFlow has a distributed database layer with database plugins for OVSDB, Cassandra, and so on. The new database can easily be plugged into the framework. The controllers sync logical network topology databases and policy updates. The Dragonflow controllers at each compute node map this policy data and translates it into the OpenFlow pipeline into OVS.

Functionality supported by agents in reference Neutron implementation is implemented as an *App* in the Dragonflow controller. The controller programs the flows in OVS to redirect the matching packets to the appropriate *App* providing the service.

Let's see how DHCP is implemented as a distributed *App* in the Dragonflow implementation. The following diagram depicts the Dragonflow controller in the compute node hosting VMs. DHCP is an *App* in the local controller.

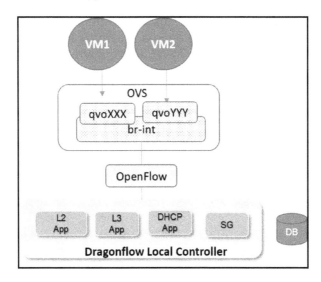

Figure 7: Neutron Dragonflow local controller with App components

The service table is programmed with the OpenFlow rule to match the source UDP port number 67. This port is the destination port of a DCHP server, and UDP port number 68 is the client requesting DHCP. The classification of the DHCP packet from the client results in action to send the DHCP_DISCOVER packet to the controller with the port's unique key metadata. The DHCP App in controller responds with DHCP_OFFER. Upon receiving DHCP_REQUEST from the client, the DHCP App populates DHCP_OPTIONS from the database and responds with DHCP_ACK.

Data Path Development Kit (DPDK)

Packet handling in Kernel has performance overheads due to interrupt handling in Kernel, data copy between Kernel and user space, system calls, and context switching. The **Data Plane Development Kit (DPDK)** provides high-performance packet processing libraries and user-space drivers for accelerated user-space data paths. The DPDK uses a run-to-completion model for enhanced network packet throughput and performance with much lower latency. It employs methods to avoid polling threads instead of interrupt processing, huge pages, multi-core processing, processor affinity, no copy from Kernel, lockless ring design with readers, and writers running on separate cores. Refer `http://dpdk.org/`.

Open vSwitch with DPDK

Open vSwitch can use the DPDK library to operate entirely in the user space as separate threads of the `vswitch` daemon (`vswitchd`).

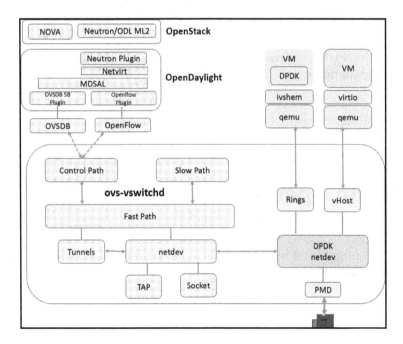

Figure 8: OVS-DPDK components

Using DPDK with OVS provides a performance boost by optimizing hotspot areas inside OVS using the DPDK packet processing libraries.

DPDK bypasses the Linux network stack and maps hardware registers to user space.

DPDK provides para-virtualized virtio **Poll Mode Drivers** (**PMD**) to access the RX and TX descriptors directly without interrupts to efficiently receive, process, and deliver packets in the user's application. Data traffic from a virtual machine is transferred to the OVS-DPDK data path and to the physical port. DPDK supports VSHMEM and user space vHost methods to communicate between guests and hosts. The `vhost` library implements a user space virtio net server allowing user application to perform packet input/output with the VM virtio net device directly. Implementation of DPDK-optimized vHost guest interface(s) allows for high-performance VM-to-VM or PHY-VM-PHY type use cases. The DPDK IVSHMEM library facilitates fast zero-copy data sharing among virtual machines (host-to-guest or guest-to-guest) by means of QEMU's IVSHMEM mechanism. Refer to: `https://gi thub.com/01org/dpdk-ovs/blob/development/docs/00_Overview.md`.

Performance tests on OVS with DPDK indicate significant improvements in packet processing over the native OVS configuration.

Open vSwitch with DPDK requires special operating system packages. For Ubuntu these DPDK package installation details are available at `https://help.ubuntu.com/16.04/serv erguide/DPDK.html`.

The steps for installing and using OVS with DPDK are available at `https://github.com/op envswitch/ovs/blob/master/INSTALL.DPDK.md`.

Neutron with Open vSwitch + DPDK

Neutron supports using Open vSwitch + DPDK vHost-user interfaces directly in the OVS ML2 driver and agent. The OVS ML2 driver will use the vHost-user VIF type when the `datapath_type` configuration is set to `netdev`. It will publish the required binding details to use OVS+DPDK and vHost-user sockets.

Refer to: `http://docs.openstack.org/developer/neutron/devref/ovs_vhostuser.htm l`.

Summary

After covering the OVS bridge interfaces in brief we showed how Neutron communicates with Open vSwitch. With OVS being the most used virtual switch in OpenStack Datacenter deployment this is important in understanding the relationship between OVS and OpenStack.

We described how Open vSwitch and Neutron are evolving to address higher performance, scaling requirements. We touched upon the scaling and performance enhancements provided by DVR, and how OVN seeks to simplify OVS Neutron integration by bringing in native supports of SDN constructs such as logical switches, routers, and ACLs. We also talked about how Dragonflow seeks to improve on the scaling and performance in certain deployment scenarios. Finally, we touched upon DPDK which significantly enhances the packet throughput by reducing the overhead of executing processing in Kernel.

Index

www.ingramcontent.com/pod-product-compliance
Lightning Source LLC
Chambersburg PA
CBHW060556060326
40690CB00017B/3728